D1514790

TREASURES OF THE
HERMITAGE

TREASURES OF THE HERMITAGE

Prehistoric Culture

Art of Classical Antiquity

Art of the Peoples of the East

Western European Art

Russian Culture

Numismatics

STUDIO EDITIONS · LONDON
AURORA ART PUBLISHERS · LENINGRAD

First published in 1987 by
Aurora Art Publishers, Leningrad
This edition published in 1990 by
Studio Editions Ltd,
Princess House, 50 Eastcastle Street,
London W1N 7AP, England

ISBN 1 85170 457 4

Printed and bound in Hong Kong

Edited by Academician BORIS PIOTROVSKY, *Director General of the Hermitage*

Prehistoric Culture

Introduction by Galina Smirnova
Notes on the plates edited by Mark Shchukin. *Notes on the plates by* Liudmila Barkova,
Liudmila Galanina, Olga Davidan, Yaroslav Damansky, Maria Zavitukhina, Irina
Zasetskaya, Natalia Kachalova, Natalia Kershner-Gorbunova, Alexander Mikliayev,
Yelena Oyateva, and Yuri Piotrovsky

Art of Classical Antiquity

Introduction by Xenia Gorbunova
Notes on the plates by Irina Saverkina

Art of the Peoples of the East

Introduction by Tatyana Arapova
Notes on the plates by Adel Adamova, Tatyana Arapova, Glafira Balashova,
Tatyana Grek, Natalia Dyakonova, Yevgeny Zeimal, Tamara Zeimal,
Anatoly Ivanov, Anna Ierusalimskaya, Gennady Leonov, Vladimir Lukonin,
Boris Marshak, Maria Pchelina, Sergei Sorokin, and Ninel Yankovskaya

Western European Art

Introduction by Irina Novosselskaya
Notes on the plates by Sergei Androsov, Boris Asvarishch, Nina Biriukova,
Kira Butler, Maria Varshavskaya, Svetlana Vsevolozhskaya, Irina Grigoryeva,
Yulia Kagan, Liudmila Kagané, Asya Kantor-Gukovskaya, Nina
Kosareva, Albert Kostenevich, Marta Kryzhanovskaya, Yuri Kuznetsov, Tatyana
Kustodieva, Irina Linnik, Marina Lopato, Charmian Mezentseva, Olga Mikhailova,
Inna Nemilova, Nikolai Nikulin, Yelizaveta Renne, and Tamara Fomichova

Russian Culture

Introduction by Galina Komelova
Notes on the plates by Avgusta Pobedinskaya and Irina Ukhanova

Numismatics

Introduction by Vsevolod Potin
Notes on the plates by Vladimir Brabich, Igor Dobrovolsky, Yuri Diukov, Nina
Ivochkina, Vsevolod Potin, Marianna Severova, Irina Sokolova, Marina Sotnikova,
and Yevgeniya Shchukina

Designed by Leonid Zykov

Translated from the Russian by Valery Dereviaghin *and* Frith Mayer

Managing editor Alla Malkova

The Hermitage in Leningrad, one of the world's outstanding museums, has been collecting and researching treasures of culture and art of various civilizations, peoples, and countries for more than two centuries.

The Museum's foundation dates to 1764. Already in its first decade, the Hermitage had impressed its rare visitors with its splendour and wealth and, according to contemporaries, had earned itself a prominent position among picture galleries collecting works by masters of world painting.

In the late eighteenth century, to accommodate the Museum's growing collection, a new building, the Small Hermitage, was constructed. This building constructed by Vallin de La Mothe consisted of two pavilions, southern and northern, with a garden suspended between them, along the sides of which later two galleries for pictures were added. The northern pavilion was intended to be a "place of solitude", resembling the park pavilions called "hermitages"; its walls were hung with pictures. "The Hermitage" was the name Catherine the Great gave the whole collection of paintings, antiquities, porcelain and cut gems housed in various parts of the Winter Palace and the buildings attached to it. The Museum has retained this name to the present day.

The collections grew and before long another building, designed by the architect Yuri Velten, was erected next to the Small Hermitage. This came to be called the Old Hermitage.

The reproductions in the Museum of Raphael's celebrated Loggias from the original in the Vatican Palace was a significant event in the cultural life of Russian society of the time. Catherine the Great wrote to Melchior Grimm in Paris: "I give Saint Raphael my solemn vow to build a gallery of his loggias by all means." The artist Christopher Unterberger was commissioned to copy the Vatican paintings and Quarenghi, having completed work on the Hermitage Theatre, set about designing a gallery to shelter the copied paintings. The project required ten years for completion: only in 1788 were the canvases with the replicas mounted in the newly-constructed building.

At the beginning of the nineteenth century the first "decree" on the Museum's structure was issued, calling for the division of the Hermitage into five departments and establishment of a museum restoration school.

In 1812 the war with France disrupted the regular course of life at the Hermitage. Upon the invasion of Russia by Napoleon's army, the Museum's priceless treasures were ordered on a "secret expedition". The only mention of their evacuation and subsequent return in 1813 was in court records.

To commemorate Russia's 1812 victory in the Great Patriotic War a special gallery was designed by the architect Carlo Rossi in the Winter Palace for portraits of Russian generals, analogous to the Windsor Castle gallery where portraits of those who participated in the battle of Waterloo hang. The English painter George Dawe, with the assistance of Russian artists Wilhèlm Golicke and Alexander Poliakov, painted 329 portraits for this gallery.

A fire in 1837 destroyed the interior decor of the Winter Palace but the Museum itself was saved. It became obvious in the course of restoration of the palace that the collection was cramped in the existing space and it was high time to expand the facilities. The New Hermitage, the first special museum repository, intended to accomodate all the collections, was designed by Leo von Klenze, who built the Munich Alte Pinakothek. The Russian architects Vasily Stasov and Nikolai Yefimov headed the commission which executed the project.

The appearance of the interiors of the "Public Museum", as the New Hermitage was called, has been faithfully reproduced in contemporary watercolours by Eduard Hau and Louis Premazzi.

Gradually the Hermitage began to take on the character of a museum institution, although it remained under the palace administration right up to the October Revolution of 1917.

Soon after the revolution, on October 5, 1918, the Council of People's Commissars issued a decree regarding the protection of art and antique relics. Lenin more than once pointed out that the construction of a socialist society cannot be carried out without utilizing the cultural values accumulated by humanity throughout its history. A state museum reserve was created to divide the nationalized private art collections and oversee the museums' activities. The Hermitage collections received through it many works which filled in previously existing gaps, especially in nineteenth-century art.

In 1930 and 1931 the work of the Hermitage was reorganized: the Museum's structure was reviewed and its exhibitions modified. The changes were aimed at arranging exhibits on a more exact historical basis. Systematic research of the collections and compilation of their scientific inventories were undertaken and the scope of restoration work was widened significantly. Exchanges of exibits with foreign museums were resumed. The Hermitage's developing and diversifying activities were interrupted by World War II, when its collections were evacuated far away, to the Urals. The museum personnel who accompanied the collections to the hinterland continued their work there, while those who stayed in Leningrad during the siege strove to keep the museum buildings safe as well as to preserve intact pieces left in the city. Only in October 1945 was it possible to return the evacuated treasures to their home in the Hermitage and begin reconstruction and expansion of the exhibitions.

Today, the Hermitage collections consist of some three million pieces which are exhibited in 353 rooms occupying five buildings—the Winter Palace, Small Hermitage, Large (or Old) Hermitage, Hermitage Theatre, and New Hermitage—created by the eminent architects Bartolomeo Francesco Rastrelli, Vallin de La Mothe, Yuri Velten, Giacomo Quarenghi, and Leo von Klenze. The Museum's six departments boast works of art and cultural relics dating from ancient times to the present day.

The most ancient artifacts found on the territory of the Soviet Union are preserved and studied in the Department of Prehistoric Culture. Especially worthy of mention are the antiquities of the Scythian world. The Scythians, nomadic tribes living on the steppes along the northern coast of the Black Sea between the seventh and third centuries B.C., created splendid works of art. Fine Scythian goldwork is world-famous.

The Department of Classical Antiquity is renowned for its collection of Greek and Roman sculpture, painted antique vases, cut gems, and jewellery. Particularly interesting are the collections of Roman portrait sculpture, Tanagra terra-cottas, the rich gem collection, and materials excavated from former Greek and Roman colonies in the Northern Black Sea Coast region. The burial mounds of the Scythian aristocracy have yielded numerous gold and silver articles produced by the Greeks. Every year the Museum's collections are enriched by the discoveries of archaeological expeditions.

The Department of the East houses relics from the ancient civilizations of Egypt and Mesopotamia, Asia Minor and Iran, Turkey, India, Mongolia, China, and Japan. The most representative and constantly growing collections in the department are those of the eastern countries which are now part of the Soviet Union—the Central Asian and Transcaucasian republics.

The Department of Russian Culture preserves and exhibits materials dating from early Slavic times to the second half of the nineteenth century: Old Russian icons, portraits, watercolours, pencil drawings, lithographs, and objects of applied art (porcelain, glass, stone, metal, jewellery, costumes, carpets, and tapestries). The interiors of the Winter Palace also belong to this department; in many of its rooms the decor is still preserved as it was created by the foremost Russian masters in the mid-nineteenth century.

The Department of Numismatics owns a collection of coins, orders, and medals from different countries and periods, of which any world museum would be proud. Its treasures include unique coins and some of the most illustrious orders and medals in the world. This collection, which has been accumulating numismatic material for over two centuries, now numbers about 1,100,000 items.

Most famous of all the Hermitage departments is the Department of Western European Art, comprising a picture gallery and collections of sculpture and decorative arts. In the celebrated picture gallery the core of the Hermitage art collection, hang masterpieces of world painting from the fourteenth through the twentieth century. The canvases by the foremost artists of Italy, Spain, Flanders, Holland, France, Germany, and England as well as sculptures, pencil drawings, and works of applied art, including Limoges enamel, Spanish glass, French jewellery, German porcelain, Belgian tapestries, and engraved gems from various countries—all examples of consummate skill—have won the Museum international acclaim.

In 1964, when the Hermitage celebrated its bicentennial, it was awarded the Soviet State's highest decoration, the Order of Lenin, for its significant contribution to cultural work.

The Hermitage maintains close ties with different art museums of the world. In recent years, it has hosted exhibits from European countries, Asia, and America. This activity is an important factor favourable for strengthening cultural and scientific ties between nations and for mutual understanding and friendship between peoples.

Boris Piotrovsky,
Academician,
Director General of the Hermitage

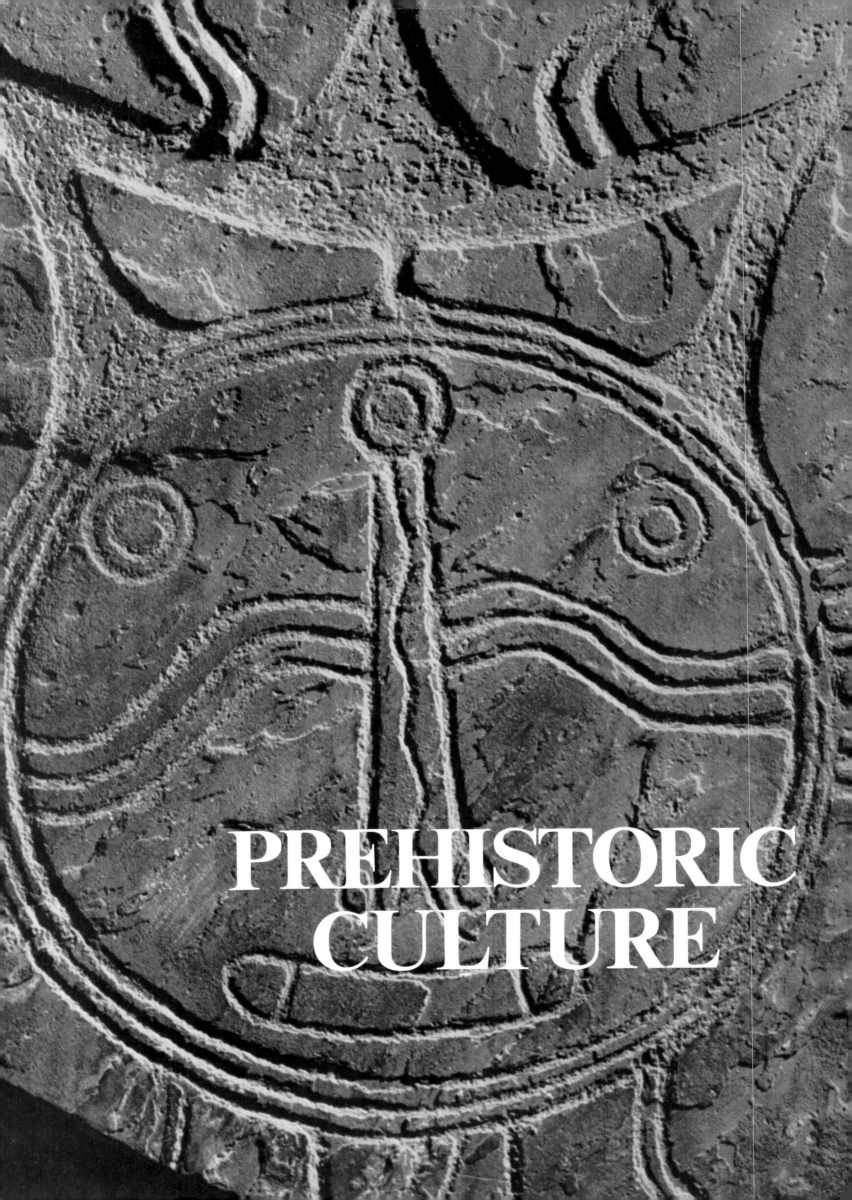

PREHISTORIC CULTURE

The greater part of the Hermitage's fabulous collection of archaeological relics, over 450 thousand items, is concentrated in its Department of Prehistoric Culture. These articles encompass an immense historic period in the lives of the peoples who inhabited the present-day territory of the USSR, from the West Bug and Prut rivers in the west to the Pacific coast in the east, from the shores of the Black Sea and the foothills of the Tien Shan in the south to the Taimyr peninsula in the north, a period lasting from the Stone Age to the birth of the Russian state.

The collection had its beginnings in the early nineteenth century, when a magnificent assortment of gold and silver articles discovered in 1812 in a rich burial vault near the village of Conceşti on the right bank of the Prut entered the Museum. In the mid-nineteenth century the oldest archaeological collection in Russia, the so-called Siberian collection of Peter the Great which consisted of over 250 gold ornaments unearthed in the late seventeenth and early eighteenth centuries from ancient barrows in Western Siberia and Kazakhstan, was transferred to the Hermitage from the *Kunstkammer*, the first Russian public museum. Many of the finds were melted down into ingots and thus irretrievably lost, but a significant part of the trove came into the possession of the Ural industrialist Nikita Demidov who presented it to Catherine, Peter the Great's spouse. Peter the Great fully appreciated the objects' artistic worth and ordered the acquisition by the Kunstkammer of all similar finds in the future. This was the beginning of the Hermitage's unique collection of art relics from the sixth to the first century B.C.—cast gold plaques that adorned the clothes, *grivnas* (crescent-shaped neck ornaments), bracelets and parts of horses' harness with depictions of fighting animals, as well as other brilliant works of art.

However, the bulk of this collection of ancient gold was the product of systematic excavations conducted in Russia in the second half of the nineteenth century. An Imperial Archaeological Comission was set up in 1859, and this body handed over to the Hermitage all especially valuable finds unearthed in barrows and burial vaults in the Northern Black Sea Coast region and the North Caucasus. It is from this source that the Museum received one of its proudest possessions—a collection of Scythian and Sarmatian goldwork that has no equal for its fullness, variety, and artistic merit. Among the most noteworthy are finds from such well-known barrows of Scythian and Sarmatian nobles as the Kelermes and Ulsky in the North Caucasus, the Solokha and Chertomlyk on the Dniester river, and the Khokhlach barrow near the city of Novocherkassk. There are relics of earlier periods too, and of these the most striking are those from the Maikop barrow complex with its extremely rare samples of metalwork from the third millennium B.C. and artistic bronzes pertaining to the Koban culture of the late Bronze Age.

Also acquired at the end of the last century was a huge hoard of precious metal objects, unearthed near the village of Malaya Pereshchepina in Poltava Province, as well as treasure-troves of ancient Russian origin—the Gnezdovsky, Nevelsky, and other hoards which contain many interesting examples of the jeweller's art of those days.

After the October Revolution, in the 1920s, the Museum's archaeological collections were augmented by relics from nationalized private collections. The Department of Antiquities was reorganized into the present Department of Prehistoric Culture on the Territory of the USSR whose stocks numbered about twenty thousand items. The new department focused its activities on classifying all exhibits according to the basic periods in the history of the peoples who inhabited the territory of the USSR in ancient times.

In the 1930s–1950s the department's stocks were significantly enlarged with the transfer to the Hermitage of the Russian Museum's archaeological collections, numerous relics discovered by the well-known Russian archaeologist Nikolai Brandenburg (formerly housed in the Artillery Museum) and several collections from other museums and institutes in Leningrad and Moscow.

But the source that in the last fifty years contributed most to the department's stocks were archaeological expeditions organized by the Hermitage, the Institute of Archaeology of the USSR Academy of Sciences, and Leningrad University.
A number of acquisitions from this source deserve special mention, for example the gold items from the Chilikta barrow in Kazakhstan and the gold ornaments from rich burial mounds near the villages of Kalinovka and Verkhneye Pogromnoye in the Lower Volga region. These were an important addition to the department's collection of Scythian and Sarmatian gold. The department's collection of jewellery from the fourth to the seventh century A.D., begun in the nineteenth century, was augmented with valuable finds from the same Verkhneye Pogromnoye burial mound and from another near the village of Tugozvonovo in the Altai mountains.

Known the world over are the Scythian relics found in the Altai mountains, at the Shibeh, Bashadar, and Pazyryk sites and near the village of Tuekta: these wooden, fur, felt, and leather articles uncovered in a well-preserved state because of the permafrost in the barrow's compartments. Among the items extracted from the permafrost layer were some carpets, definitely the oldest in existence, clothes, footwear, a chariot, various implements, musical instruments, and other articles made by the nomads of the Altai almost 2,500 years ago.

In 1969 the department received another consignment of finds in perfect condition. These came from a first-century B.C. entombment discovered in the Oglakhty mountains in the middle reaches of the Yenisei river in which the corpses were clad in fur clothing and had their faces covered with painted gypsum masks. The wooden vault also contained two human-sized dolls in fur coats, a fur quiver trimmed with silk, and earthenware vessels.

The pre-Scythian and Scythian collections of the department were significantly expanded with the entry of materials unearthed by the West Ukraine Expedition. Finds from the multilayer settlement of Magala (fourteenth to eighth century B.C.) and a rich assortment of grave goods from seventh- and sixth-century B.C. barrows near the villages of Kruglik, Doliniany, and Perebykovtsy enabled the Hermitage to display for the first time the culture of the Dniester group of Scythian tribes that inhabited the forest-and-steppe regions of the country. Another expedition, to the

Polesye region in Byelorussia, helped fill in the lacunae in the Museum's collection of items relating to the Zarubintsy culture, whereas the ongoing Ferghana expedition each year supplies the department with materials unearthed in settlements and tombs of the first few centuries A.D.

In recent years the department's collection of Caucasian antiquities has been augmented by two rich sets of Caucasian bronzes. One of them consists of first-rate finds which illustrate the Colchian culture of the transition period from the Bronze to the Iron Age.

In all, during the Soviet period the Department of Prehistoric Culture has had its collections increased twentyfold. All the materials are grouped into nine sections organized on the geographical and chronological principles. The finest specimens make up one of the Hermitage's permanent exhibitions—The Culture and Art of Primitive Societies on the Territory of the USSR. Objects made of gold and other precious metals are displayed in the Hermitage's Gold Room.

The exhibits on permanent display constitute but a fraction of the department's vast archaeological collection, which is the subject of ceaseless study by specialists and enjoys world renown. In the last few years it has been shown in Bulgaria, Czechoslovakia, the Federal Republic of Germany, Finland, France, the German Democratic Republic, Great Britain, Holland, Hungary, Italy, Japan, Mexico, Poland, Switzerland, the USA, and Yugoslavia.

Galina Smirnova

1. Birds

Mammoth tusk. Length 11.8; 10.3 cm
Paleolithic. 20th millennium B.C.
Ancient site of Malta, Irkutsk Region. Excavated by M. Gerasimov in
1928–30. Inv. Nos. 370/739; 370/740

Representations of birds are seldom encountered in objects of Paleolithic art. One of the figurines found on the site of Malta resembles a swan in flight. A similar find in a child's burial suggests that these figurines, head down, were worn as pectoral amulets.

2. Fish

Slate. Length 30 cm
Neolithic. 3rd millennium B.C.
Verkholensk burial ground, Irkutsk Region. Excavated by A. Okladnikov
in 1951. Inv. No. 1791/1

The figure carved out of greenish slate resembles some species of the salmon family. Due to a hole located strictly in the centre the figurine retains the horizontal position when suspended. Apparently it was used as a decoy in harpoon fishing. Representations of this kind are characteristic of the Neolithic Age in the Lake Baikal area and the upper reaches of the Lena.

3. Binocular-shaped vessel

Clay. Height 21.5 cm
Eneolithic. Tripolye culture. Second half of the 3rd millennium B.C.
Ancient site near Polivanov Yar, Chernovtsy Region. Excavated by
T. Passek in 1950. Inv. No. 50/753

The vessel shaped as two bottomless cups linked by cross-pieces belongs
to ritual objects. It is adorned with elegant spiral-like ornament.

5

4. Ornamented vessel

Clay. Height 39 cm
Eneolithic. Tripolye culture. Second half of the 3rd millennium B.C.
Ancient site near Zhury, Moldavian SSR. Excavated by S. Bibikov in 1952.
Inv. No. П-Яр 52/37

This pear-shaped vessel with a tall tapered neck and funnel-shaped rim is a typical example of Tripolye pottery of the middle period in the Ukraine and Moldavia. The ornament is executed in black and white.

5. Bullock. Decoration of a pole supporting the funeral canopy

Gold. Height 6 cm
Mid-3rd millennium B.C.
Maikop barrow (now Krasnodar Territory). Excavated by N. Veselovsky in 1897. Inv. No. 34/17

This is one of the four cast gold figurines found in a rich barrow of a chief in the North Caucasus. The round aperture served for attaching the figure to the pole.

6

6. Hairpin with a poleaxe-shaped top decorated with figures of dogs and a stag

Bronze. Height 17.7 cm
Bronze Age. Koban culture. Early 1st millennium B.C.
Gudauty, the Caucasus. Found in 1940. Inv. No. 1731/71

The Koban culture in the Central Caucasus has yielded brilliant specimens of bronzeware and weapons. The bronze objects were often decorated with symbols of the forces of Nature.

7. Rhyton terminating in a goat's head

Bronze. Height 55.5 cm
Bronze Age. Colchian culture. *Ca.* 8th century B.C.
Gudauty, the Caucasus. Found in 1940. Inv. No. 1566/9

This horn-shaped drinking vessel is adorned with engraved representations of a snake, galloping horses, and flying birds. The representations have their origin in the religious concepts of ancient inhabitants of Colchis, which was one of the centres of bronzework.

8. Idol

Copper. Height 14 cm
Bronze Age. Second half of the 2nd millennium B.C.
Kostroma Province (now Kostroma Region). Found as part of the
"Galich Hoard" in 1836. Inv. No. 77/1

The seated male figure with a disproportionately big head and narrow chest was found together with several other objects of the same kind, silver articles, and coins. The figure has nine projections radiating out from the head and shoulders. The sculptured figure was probably meant to be mounted upon a pole.

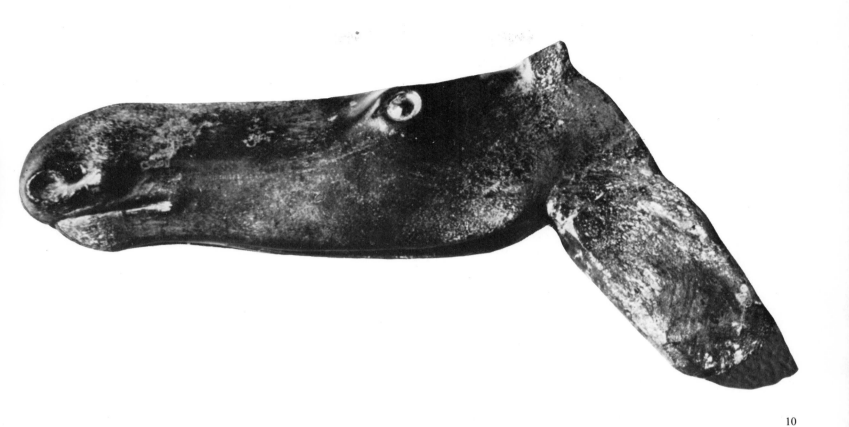

9. Seated female statuette

Clay. Height 27 cm
Eneolithic. Second half of the 4th millennium B.C.
Ancient site near Yalangach-Depe, South Turkmenia. Excavated by
I. Khlopin in 1957, 1959, or 1960. Inv. No. Ял 1–10/12

The statuette is a magnificent example of the High
Eneolithic sculpture found in Turkmenia. Typical for
it is the emphasis of sexual characteristic. The solar
signs testify to the magic role of the statuette.

10. Head of a female elk

Elk antler. Length 19.5 cm
Bronze age. 2nd millennium B.C.
Shigir peatbog, Yekaterinburg Province (now Sverdlovsk Region). Ex-
cavated by V. Tolmachov in 1910/1914. Inv. No. 5546/365

One of the best examples of Neolithic and Bronze Age
sculpture. The head of the animal is rendered with a
high degree of realism. The surface is highly polished
(probably the result of frequent use). The sculpture
apparently was a decoration of a handle of some vessel
or of a ritual staff.

11

11. Belt buckle with geometrical and animal ornament

Bronze. Length 17.2 cm
Bronze Age. Koban culture. First half of the 1st millennium B.C.
North Ossetia, the Caucasus. The D. Vyrubova collection. Inv. No. 1739/2

The belt buckle shaped as an elongated quadrangle is ornamented with three openwork figures of dogs alternating with a geometrical pattern.

12. Seated female statuette

Clay. Height 19 cm
Eneolithic. Early 3rd millennium B.C.
Ancient site near Kara-Depe, South Turkmenia. Excavated by V. Masson in 1955–57 or 1960. Inv. No. 415/129

The statuette pertains to the Late Eneolithic period. The bird-like head, square shoulders, and the use of applied decoration testify to the influence of the art of ancient Mesopotamia.

13. Slab with representation of a fantastic animal

Sandstone. Length 140 cm
Bronze Age. Okunevo culture. First half of the 2nd millennium B.C.
Chernovaya VIII burial ground, Krasnoyarsk Territory. Excavated by G. Maximenkov in 1962.
Inv. No. 2441/2

It is probable that the fantastic three-eyed beast with antlers and a three-pronged crown symbolizes the ancestress and protectress of the family.

14. Decoration of a throne arm with heads of lions and rams, and with flower buds

Gold and amber. Length 19.2 cm
Scythian period. 7th–6th century B.C.
Kelermes barrow, the North Caucasus (now Krasnodar Territory).
Excavated by D. Schulz in 1903. Inv. No. Ky 1904 1/11

One of the twin decorations with grooves on the back, apparently for attaching to a throne arm. Heads of lions and rams are often represented in the art of the Ancient East. The modelled forms are combined with granulated decoration and ornamental patterns resembling the *cloisonné* technique.

15. Stag

Gold. Length 31.5 cm
Scythian period. Early 6th century B.C.
Kostromskaya barrow, the North Caucasus (now Krasnodar Territory).
Excavated by N. Veselovsky in 1897. Inv. No. Ky 1897 1/1

Massive, large, and made in high relief, the figure of a stag belongs to most impressive specimens of the early Scythian Animal Style. The figure was used as a decoration of an iron shield.

16. Panther

Gold. Length 32.6 cm
Scythian period. Early 7th–6th century B.C.
Kelermes barrow, the North Caucasus (now Krasnodar Territory).
Excavated by D. Schulz in 1903. Inv. No. Ky 1903 2/1

The plaque belongs to most accomplished specimens of the early Scythian Animal Style. It was used for decorating a shield.

17, 18. Comb

Gold. Height 12.3 cm
Scythian period. Late 5th–early 4th century B.C.
Solokha barrow, steppes of the Dnieper area. Excavated by N. Veselovsky in 1913. Inv. No. Дн 1913 1/1

The gold comb is a remarkable work of art of the Scythian period. Its top is adorned with a frieze of five recumbent lions; these are surmounted with a sculptured group of Scythian warriors in combat. The master fully conveyed the drama of a fierce fight. The precision of detail gives a clear idea of the Scythians' appearance, and the clothing and weapons they used. This imparts the comb a documentary evidence.

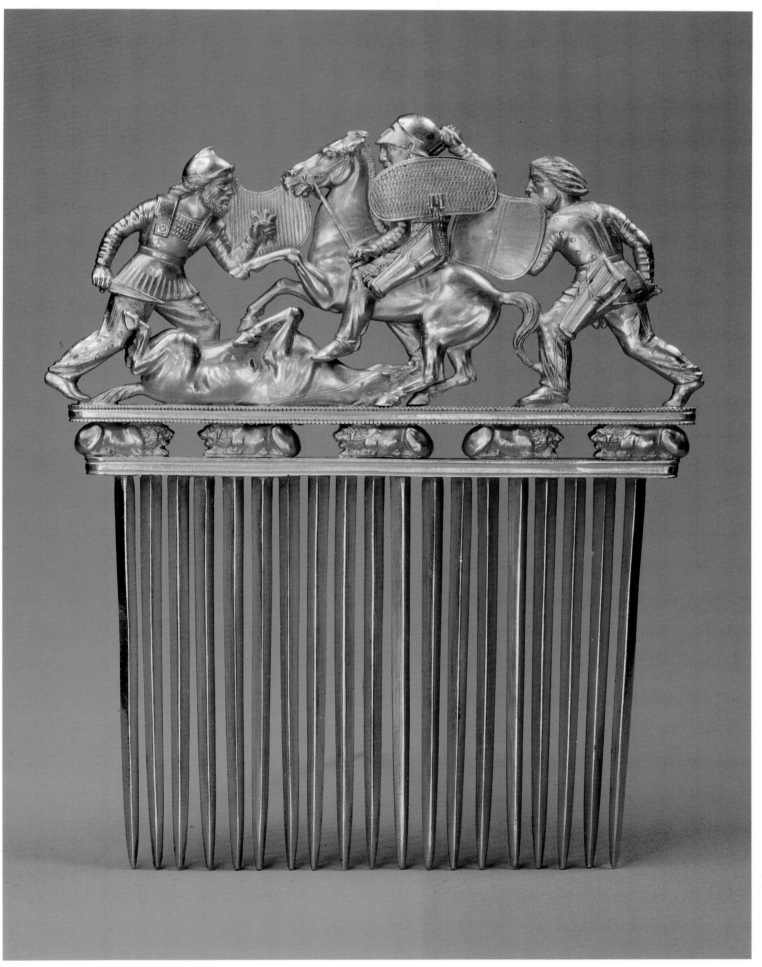

17, 18 ▶

19

19. Handle of a sword

Gold and iron. Length 21.9 cm
Scythian period. 5th–4th century B.C.
Chertomlyk barrow, the Ukraine (now Dnepropetrovsk Region).
Excavated by N. Zabelin in 1863. Inv. No. Дн 1863 1/448

The handle of an iron sword with a gold mounting is ornamented in a manner reminiscent of the Achaemenid period. Elements of this style can be glimpsed in the heads of the bulls and in the low-relief compositions with groups of horsemen hunting.

20. Finial with figure of a stag

Bronze. Height 15.3 cm
Scythian period. 4th century B.C.
Chmyriova Mogila, the Ukraine (now Zaporozhye Region). Excavated by
F. Brown in 1898. Inv. No. Дн 1898 1/328

The finial with a sculptured figure of a stag is in the style of late Scythian
art, which is characterized by an emphatically ornamental treatment of
figures.

22. Finial shaped as a griffin holding a stag's head in its beak

Wood and leather. Height 9.8 cm
5th–4th century B.C.
Pazyryk II barrow, Altai mountains. Excavated by S. Rudenko in 1947.
Inv. No. 1684/176

This finial is a brilliant example of the Scytho-Siberian Animal style. The main motif of fighting animals reflected the mythology of the ancient population of the Altai area. Wood was usually employed in combination with leather. The wings, the ears, and the crest of the griffin are of leather. The stag's antlers are also of leather, each tine terminating in a rooster's head on a long neck. The purpose of the object is not clear.

21. Saddle cover

Felt, leather, and horse hair. Length 120 cm
5th–4th century B.C.
Pazyryk I barrow, Altai mountains. Excavated by M. Griaznov in 1929.
Inv. No. 1295/150

The motif of a winged griffin standing on a thrown down ibex is common in Scytho-Siberian art. The cover is brightly dyed, which adds to its decorative quality.

23. Finial shaped as a griffin holding stag's head in its beak

Wood and leather. Height 27 cm
5th–4th century B.C.
Pazyryk II barrow, Altai mountains. Excavated by S. Rudenko in 1947. Inv. No. 1684/170

The griffin motif, borrowed from the art of the Near East, was organically absorbed by the Altai culture. The griffin then was a symbol of strength and power.

23

24. Finial with three birds

Bronze. Height 28.9 cm
Scythian period. Early 3rd century B.C.
Alexandropol barrow, the Ukraine (now Dnepropetrovsk Region). Found in 1851. Inv. No. Дн 1851 1/17

The finial is shaped as a trident with sculptured figures of birds holding bells in their beaks. Rather laconic in manner, this artifact of the late Scythian period resembles earlier specimens of the Animal Style.

25. Small table with carved legs

Wood. Height 36.7 cm
5th–4th century B.C.
Pazyryk II barrow, Altai mountains. Excavated by S. Rudenko in 1947. Inv. No. 1684/35

This dismountable table illustrates the kind of household articles in use with the early nomad tribes in the Altai area. The table-top, made of a single block of wood, was painted in cinnabar-red, still visible on its underside. The legs are shaped as rampant tigers.

26. Plaque with a tiger and a fantastic wolf fighting

Gold. Length 16.8 cm
Sakian period. 7th–6th century B.C.
Siberian collection of Peter the Great. Received in 1716. Inv. No. Си 1727 1/12

This dynamic composition showing the fighting of a tiger with a fantastic wolf is embossed in relief on the cast gold plaque.

27, 28 ▶

27, 28. Belt buckle with a scene of animals fighting

Gold with turquoise and coral inlays. Length 19.5 cm
4th–3rd century B.C.
Siberian collection of Peter the Great. Received in 1716. Inv. No. Си 1727 1/2

One of a pair of solid gold buckles from the Siberian collection of Peter the Great. It presents a scene of animal combat—an eagle, a tiger, a wolf, and some fantastic beast. All details of this openwork buckle, decorated with inlays of coral and turquoise, are finely finished.

29

30

29. Finial with head of a bull

Bronze. Height 24.2 cm
Scythian period. Late 6th–early 5th century B.C.
Ulsky barrow, the North Caucasus (now Krasnodar Territory). Excavated
by N. Veselovsky in 1909. Inv. No. Ky 1909 1/108

The pear-shaped openwork finial of a hearse pole
terminates in a sculptured head of a bull. This representation originates in the art of the Ancient East,
where the bull was regarded as a symbol of the cult of
the Sun and fertility.

30. Chaser with figure of a moufflon

Bronze. Height 7.5 cm
Sakian period. 7th–6th century B.C.
Lake Borovoye, North Kazakhstan. Inv. No. 2133/1

Representations of a moufflon standing with its four
feet drawn together are often encountered in Kazakhstan, South Siberia, and Central Asia. Realistic treatment of forms is characteristic of the earlier specimens
of the Animal Style found in Central Asia.

31. Vessel with an elk-shaped handle

Gold, inlaid with turquoise. Height 7.5 cm
Sarmatian period. 1st century A.D.
Khokhlach barrow (now Rostov Region). Found in 1864 as part of the
"Novocherkassk treasure". Inv. No. 2213/13

The elk is depicted in the Sarmatian Animal Style.
Turquoise and coral inlays were often employed by
local craftsmen to emphasize the eyes and nostrils of
animals and to convey the muscles. The vessel was
discovered in one of the richest Sarmatian burials.

32. Bear-shaped handle of a vessel

Bronze. Length 27 cm
Perm Animal Style. *Ca.* 1st–4th century A.D.
Village of Yekaterinovka (now Perm Region). Found in 1900.
Inv. No. 579/1

The fantastic animal has a human body and head and
paws of some big wild beast. The five-toed paws and
the bulging muzzle with smallish eyes in deep eye-
sockets allow to identify it as a bear. Instead of ears
the animal has two teardrop-shaped holes. The bronze
bear cast into a one-side mould could have been used
as a handle of some sort of vessel or as part of applied
decoration.

32

33

33, 34. Bracelet

Gold, garnets, and paste. Diameter 8.6 cm
Hunnish period. 4th–5th century A.D.
Taman peninsula (now Krasnodar Territory). Found in 1854.
Inv. No. 2070/1

This impressive bracelet made of thick gold wire belongs to the Hunnish period. At each end is a head of a snarling beast of prey, probably a wolf. The eyes, ears, nostrils, and withers are emphasized with garnet inlays.

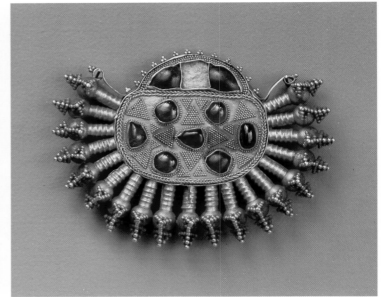

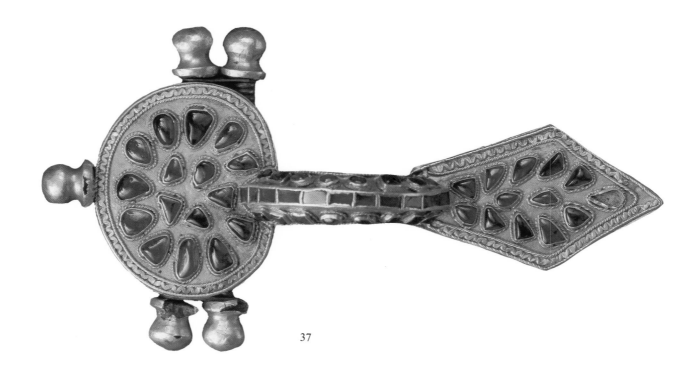

37

35, 36. *Kolt* pendant

Gold and garnets. Length 8.6 cm
Hunnish period. 4th–5th century A.D.
Village of Verkhne-Yablochny (now Volgograd Region). Found in 1902.
Inv. No. 1948/1

This fine example of a *kolt,* or temple pendant, is shaped like a disk with rays around it. The obverse is richly ornamented with garnet inlays and granulated patterns, while the reverse carries a ritual subject: the "Tree of Life" with a figure of a bird on top and holy animals surrounding it. The *kolt* illustrates the polychrome style of the Hunnish period.

37. Fibula

Gold, silver, and garnets. Length 13.8 cm
Hunnish period. Late 4th–5th century A.D.
Nezhin (now Chernigov Region). Found in 1873. Inv. No. 2117/1

This decorative clasp is inlaid with garnets. On the outer rim is a border of notched wire and a narrow ornamental band. The clasp belongs to the artifacts of the polychrome style of the Hunnish period.

54

38

39, 40

38. Temple ring

Silver. Diameter 7.8 cm
10th century A.D.
Volhynia (now Rovno Region). Found in 1883 as part of the "Borshchev-sky Treasure". Inv. No. 1017/11

The temple ring, one of a pair, is embellished with an openwork crescent and figured beads. The granulation technique predominates in its decor. Ornaments of this type are generally referred to as "Volhynian ear-rings", from the name of the region where they are most often to be found.

39, 40. *Kolt* pendant

Gold and enamel. Diameter 3.6 cm
11th–12th century
Alexandrovskaya Square, Chernigov (now Ukrainian SSR). Found in 1887. Inv. No. 1021/9

On one side of the *kolt* is the representation of a young saint holding a cross in his right hand. On the other side is a tree on a rectangular stand. Both representa-tions are executed in *cloisonné* enamel.

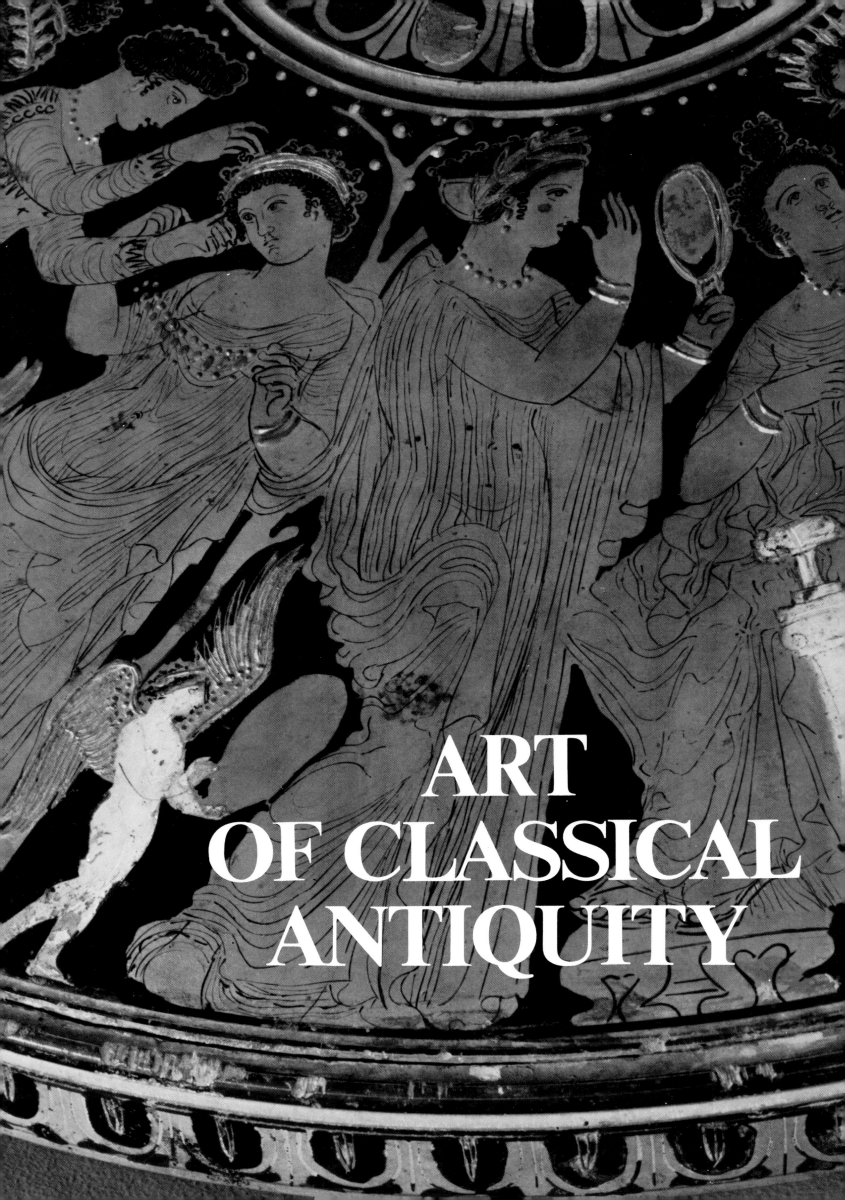

ART
OF CLASSICAL
ANTIQUITY

The Hermitage's Department of Classical Antiquity was organized in the mid-nineteenth century. By that time the Museum's collection of antique art had grown to such proportions that it took up the entire ground floor of the then just completed New Hermitage building.

The art of classical antiquity was collected in Russia as early as the first half of the eighteenth century, and most of the items that entered the Hermitage Museum at its inception came from the St. Petersburg palaces of the royal family and the nobility, and from the Academy of Arts. For example, one of the first antique statues to appear in Russia, *Venus of Tauride*, was originally installed in Peter the Great's Summer Gardens, and later adorned the interior of Prince Potiomkin's Tauride Palace. It was acquired in 1720 in exchange for the relics of St. Bridget, a Catholic saint.

Several extremely valuable acquisitions were made by the Museum in the second half of the eighteenth and first half of the nineteenth century—from Lyde Brown a collection of sculptures, from the Duke of Orleans a gem collection, from Doctor Pizzati the Greek vases, bronzes, and terra-cottas he had collected in Italy.

In 1834 the Pizzati collection arrived from Rome, and formed the nucleus of the Hermitage collection of painted vases, bronzes, and terra-cottas. In the 1850s the collection of sculpture was greatly enriched by a number of new additions: *The Resting Satyr* and *Athena* (by sculptors of Phidias's circle) from the collection of the Urals industrialists, the Demidovs; and forty-six sculptures from the Laval collection, including a magnificent bust of Emperor Balbinus.

In 1861–62 the Hermitage acquired a large part of the fabulous Campana collection — 787 items, comprising a large number of Italic vases, bronzes, and sculptures. Many of the vases in the collection had been skilfully restored, and some of them even reconstructed, but in those days their authenticity was not questioned. It was only after thorough investigation that scholars have managed to identify the original parts and restore the authentic designs. In 1884 the Museum received a group of Tanagra statuettes and carved gems from Piotr Saburov, the Russian ambassador to Berlin.

During the first three decades of the nineteenth century the Hermitage began to benefit from a new and very important source—archaeological expeditions. Discovered in 1830 near Kerch (on the site of Panticapaeum, the ancient capital of the Bosporan Kingdom) was the Kul-Oba barrow. The riches it yielded, the abundance of gold ornaments among the finds encouraged archaeologists and their sponsors to pursue their exploration further. From that time on all the finest relics unearthed by archaeological expeditions on the territories of the Crimea (ancient Tauride) and the Taman peninsula were handed over to the Hermitage, which thus gradually amassed a magnificent collection of Grecian vases, sculptures, terra-cottas, bronzes, and various objects carved in wood and ivory. These excavations, which continue to this day, helped bring into being a unique, precisely documented collection of objects featuring the art and culture of the Northern Black Sea Coast region.

The actual composition of the collection is largely a result of the way in which it was assembled. On the one hand, the personal taste of the agents entrusted with purchasing art works at European sales played a considerable role; on the other, the artistic interests of the royal family and the nobility who followed in its footsteps, were not to be neglected. This explains the great wealth of certain sections (gems, vases, Roman portrait sculptures), and the relative incompleteness of others.

After the October Revolution of 1917 many private collections (the Shuvalov, the Stroganov, the Botkin, and others) entered the Hermitage. Although small in size, these contained some outstanding works of antique art. Suffice it to mention the magnificent vases of the Shuvalov collection painted by a miniaturist of the post-Phidias period, commonly referred to as the Master of the Shuvalov Amphora.

The department's exhibition is arranged in chronological order. Comprehensive exhibitions characterizing the evolution of art in Greece and Rome are supplemented by thematic displays. On the whole the exhibition reflects in full measure all the richness and scientific value of such groups as Grecian and Italian vases, glyptics, Roman portraiture, and blown-glass articles. A place apart belongs to relics found in the Northern Black Sea Coast region, on the site of ancient Greek colonies (Berezan, Olbia, Chersonesus, Nymphaeum, and the minor Bosporan cities). The department also has in its possession rare objects from several South Russian barrows. The richest assortments were yielded by the Seven Brothers, Kul-Oba, Yuz-Oba, Bolshaya Bliznitsa, and Artiukhovsky barrows as well as the tomb of Rhescuporis.

The South Russian section boasts a superb collection of Attic vases of the fifth and fourth centuries B.C. unequalled for quality and completeness. Especially noteworthy are the red-figure lebetes (including several by the master of Marsyas), the lecane basins from the Yuz-Oba barrow, the figured vessels from the Phanagoria burial vault, the relief-figure vases—two lecythi by Xenophantes and the famous hydria with a depiction of Athena's argument with Poseidon (the latter an invaluable historical source for reconstructing the pediment of the Parthenon), the oinochoe from the Zmeiny barrow, and others.

The department's admirable collection of wooden articles ranges from monumental sarcophagi to miniature pyxides of the utmost elegance.

The Hermitage collection of classical bronzes consists primarily of statuettes, household utensils, and horse trappings from the barrows of the Northern Black Sea Coast area. The collection contains but a few isolated specimens of monumental sculpture, of which the most outstanding is undoubtedly *Portrait of a Man*.

The collection of gold and silver items is positively fabulous both for its scope and artistic merits. They include silver vessels dating from the fifth century B.C. to the early centuries A.D. These vessels, engraved and gilt, often adorned with relief compositions, provide a sufficiently comprehensive picture of the evolution of the silversmith's art in the Classic, Hellenistic, and Roman periods.

The jewellery in the department's collection is rich in variety too. Beginning with items produced in Asia Minor in the sixth century B.C. the jewelled articles on display reflect this art's most fruitful period—the fifth and fourth centuries B.C.

There are exquisite pieces by Greek masters—ear-rings from Kul-Oba, Theodosia, and Chersonesus—and beautiful items by the so-called Bosporan masters (from the Seven Brothers, Kul-Oba and Nymphaeum barrows), to cite a few examples.

The Hellenistic and Roman sections are very rich too.

The Hermitage has a superb collection of Roman portrait busts, including several works of world renown. The art of portraiture in the period from the first to the third century is illustrated by a wide range of work reflecting different stages in the development of Roman art at the time of its flowering.

The superlative technical achievements of the Antonine period are still in evidence in the portrait bust of Balbinus. But instead of the strictly structural modelling of the face, with its smooth surface, delicately worked over, here the forms are highly elusive due to the play of light and shade on the differently textured marble. This produces the effect of showing not so much the firm, already established traits of the man's character as a succession of moods reflecting the complex nature of the old senator, philosopher and scholar, his innate *joie de vivre*, undermined by a growing awareness of his own helplessness as a statesman. This work is a masterpiece of the Roman psychological portrait at the time of its most brilliant flowering in the second quarter of the third century.

No less remarkable, although belonging to a different artistic trend, is the almost contemporaneous bust of Emperor Philip the Arab in which the expressive effect is achieved by broad rather than detailed modelling, by the accentuation of basic forms, and by the deliberately coarse and simplified treatment of the marble. Only a more careful examination can reveal the complexity of character which is not seen at first glance. This is a superb example of the new type of official portrait that arose during the period of the crisis of the principate as a political institution.

In all, the value and significance of the archaeological finds lie not only in their high artistic merits, but also in the fact that they are so precisely dated.

The works of antique art selected for the present volume include masterpieces of vase-painting, glyptics, portrait sculpture, and jewellery. They reflect all the wealth and unique qualities of the Hermitage collection of antique art.

Xenia Gorbunova

41. Jug

Ionia. 640s B.C.
Pottery. Height 27 cm
Received in 1870 (found in the Temir-Gora barrow near Kerch).
Inv. No. ТГ 12

The jug discovered in the Temir-Gora barrow is one of the earliest samples of Greek pottery found in the Northern Black Sea Coast region. The two friezes of animal figures are remarkable for the precise draughtsmanship and the diversity of the decorative motifs. The jug is one of the finest among the known pieces of Rhodian-Ionian painted pottery.

43

42. Black-figure amphora: *Grazing Deer*

Clazomenae (?), Greece. Third quarter of the 6th century B.C. Enmann class
Pottery. Height 32 cm
Received in 1914 (bought on the Taman peninsula). Inv. No. Б 3222

The town of Clazomenae stands out among the pottery-producing centres of the sixth century B.C. It is probable that the grazing deer on the upper part of the amphora body was painted by a craftsman from this town. Although stylized, the figure is very expressive.

43. Black-figure kylix (drinking cup): *Heracles and Horses of Diomedes*

Attica, Greece. *Ca.* 510 B.C. By Psiax
Pottery. Dia. 16.5 cm
Provenance unknown. Inv. No. Б-9270

The painting of the kylix shows one of the exploits of Heracles. Although the black-figure technique is distinctly decorative, the artist succeeded in conveying the expressive character of the scene.

44, 45. Red-figure psykter (wine cooler): *Hetaerae Feasting*

Attica, Greece. *Ca.* 510 B.C. By Euphronios
Pottery. Height 35.5 cm
Received in 1862 from the Campana collection, Rome. Inv. No. Б 1650

This vessel for cooling wine has a high hollow foot of cylindrical form. The psykter is one of the few surviving vases with the signature of the painter. The design is simple and well-balanced, although not quite devoid of technical errors of foreshortening. The beautiful clarity of outline, however, and a particularly careful rendering of details testifies to the high skill of Euphronios, one of the greatest vase painters of the Archaic period.

46. Red-figure pelike: *The First Swallow*

Attica, Greece. *Ca.* 510 B.C.
Pottery. Height 37.5 cm
Received in 1901 from the A. Abaza collection, St. Petersburg. Inv. No. Б 2352

The vessel belongs to the early red-figure vases. The elements of the black-figure style are still preserved in the painting: the figures are shown on a plane, without any superfluous details. The sparing use of artistic devices makes the painting exquisitely simple and expressive. The vase is famous for the genre scene represented: a man, a youth, and a boy greeting the first swallow, the harbinger of spring. The inscription conveys their conversation: "Look, there is a swallow," says the youth. "Yes, by Heracles," confirms the man, "spring has come." "Here it is," cries the boy joyfully.

47. Ear-rings: *Artemis Riding a Stag*

Greece. 5th century B.C.
Gold. Length 4.3 cm
Received in 1867 (found in the necropolis at Nymphaeum, near Kerch).
Inv. No. ГКН 2

On each ear-ring, the miniature cast figure of Artemis riding a stag is suspended from the rosette which hides the hook. The fine modelling of the figure of the goddess and the natural posture of the animal allow to refer the ear-rings to the best specimens of the famous Greek "microtechnique".

48. Black-figure hydria (three-handled jar for carrying water): *Achilles and the Body of Hector*

Attica, Greece. Early 5th century B.C.
Pottery. Height 49 cm
Group of the Leagros Painter
Received in 1834 from the Pizzati collection. Inv. No. Б 173

The vessel is painted with an episode of the Troyan war. The painting is characterized by a clear and well-balanced design. The scene may have been modelled on some wall painting of the same subject.
The austere form of the hydria and the superb mastery of its decoration make it one of the best specimens of the black-figure vases of the Leagros Group.

49

49. Cantharos

Attica, Greece. Early 5th century B.C.
Pottery. Height 18.9 cm
Received in 1862 from the Campana collection, Rome. Inv. No. Б 1814

The body of the cantharos is modelled on one side as the head of a Negress, and on the other as that of a Greek woman. The latter is treated in accordance with the rules of Archaic art. The typically Negroid features are rendered in a way that enhances the decorative effect.

50. White lecythos: *Two Figures at a Stele*

Attica, Greece. Third quarter of the 5th century B.C. The Thanatos Painter. Pottery. Height 41.5 cm
Received in 1892 (bought in the van Brantegem sale, Paris).
Inv. No. Б 2022

The lecythoi were painted in mineral pigments over a white ground and were placed in tombs as funeral offerings. The subject of the painting is in keeping with the purpose of the vessel. The figures, symmetrically placed on both sides of the stele, are drawn with a free and sure hand, with a skill characteristic of vase painters of the Classical period.

50

51. Figure vessel: *Aphrodite*

Attica, Greece. Late 5th century B.C. Pottery. Height 17 cm
Received in 1869 from the necropolis at Phanagoria, Taman peninsula.
Inv. No. Фа 1869.9

The vessel for keeping fragrant oil has the form of a statuette of Aphrodite, goddess of love and beauty. The colouring is so well preserved that the pink body of the goddess seems to be emerging from the depths of a large marine shell drifting on light blue waves. The rich head-dress and the gold necklaces add to the general decorative effect. The back side of the vessel is painted with a design in the red-figure technique.

52, 53 ▶

52, 53. Figure vessel: *Sphinx*

Attica, Greece. Late 5th century B.C. Pottery. Height 21.5 cm
Received in 1869 (found in the necropolis at Phanagoria, Taman peninsula).
Inv. No. Фа 1867.7

The vessel for keeping fragrant oil is a true masterpiece of Classical Greek art. The unique feature of the specimen is its original colouring which has been exceptionally well preserved. The back side of the vessel is painted with ornamental designs in the red-figure technique.

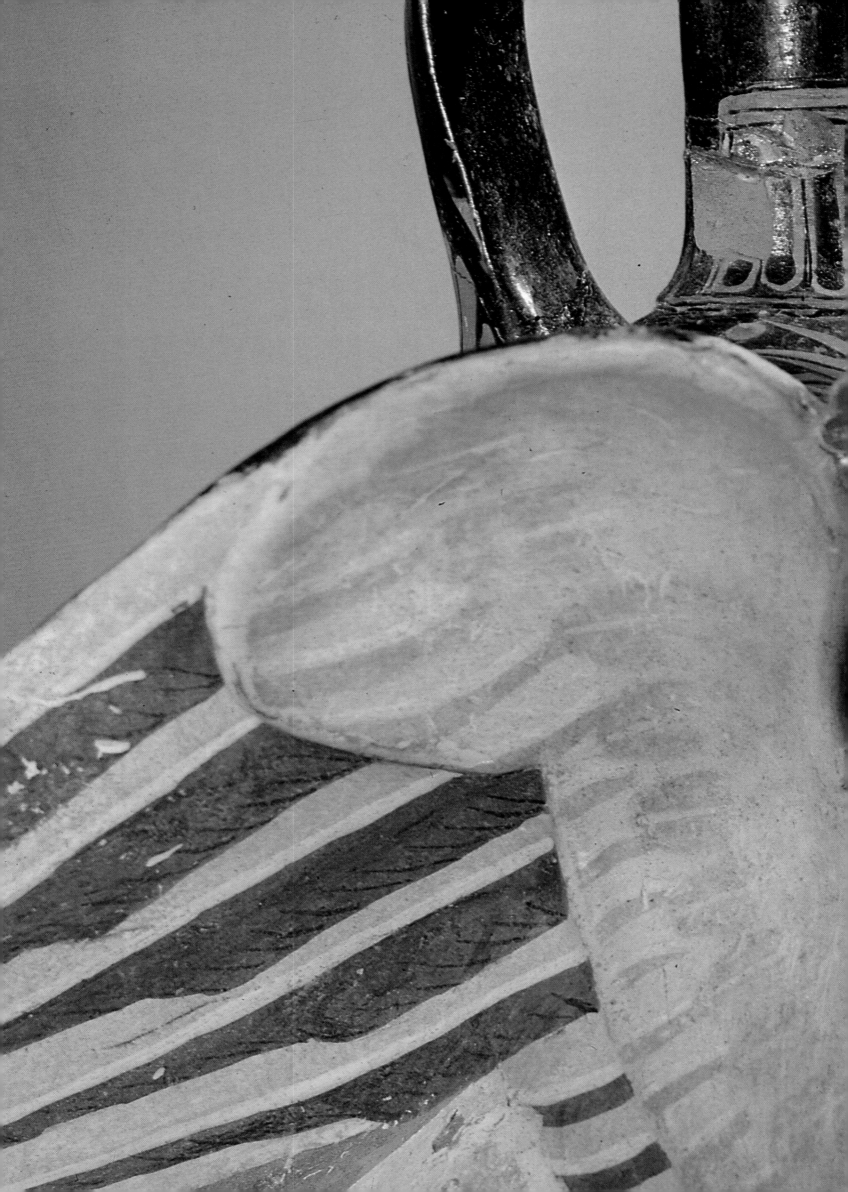

54. Stele of Philostrate

Attica, Greece. Last quarter of the 5th century B.C.
Marble. Height 41 cm
Received in 1852 from the Nesselrode collection, St. Petersburg. Inv. No. A 214

This stele is one of the best Greek tombs of the second half of the fifth century B.C. The beauty of line, the expressiveness of the gesture, the soft modelling—all these testify to the influence of Phidias.

55. Athlete

Locri, Magna Graecia. 460–450 B.C.
Bronze. Height 10.2 cm
Received in 1876 (found in the necropolis at Nymphaeum, near Kerch).
Inv. No. ГКН 91

The figure crowning a candlestick is one of the finest among the known examples of small-size bronze sculpture. It portrays a young athlete wearing the headband of victor in a gymnastic contest. The statuette was probably executed in Locri, one of the big artistic centres of Magna Graecia.

56. Procession of Demeter Worshippers

Greece. Late 5th century B.C.
Marble. Length 80 cm
Date of acquisition unknown (found in Kerch). Inv. No. ПАН 160

The subject of the relief is connected with the Eleusinian mysteries staged by the worshippers of Demeter, whose cult was very popular on the Bosporus. Its simple and austere composition is in perfect keeping with the ritual character of the relief.

57. Heracles Throttling the Nemean Lion

Roman copy after an original by Lysippus. 4th century B.C.
Marble. Height 65 cm
Received in 1887 from the F. and M. Golitsyn collection. Inv. No. A 498

The bronze original was created by Lysippus in the series devoted to the twelve labours of Heracles. The unified movement, the arrangement of figures and their bold positioning, the dynamic quality of the group give a good idea of the new methods adopted by the great sculptor in his art and of the emotional impact of his pieces.

59, 60

58. Lecythos: *Boar Hunt*

Attica, Greece. Early 4th century B.C. By Xenophantos
Pottery. Height 37 cm
Received in 1837 (found in the necropolis at Panticapaeum, Kerch).
Inv. No. П 1837.2

The lecythos is signed, which in itself is a rarity. The inscription above the frieze on the shoulders of the lecythos ("Xenophantos the Athenian made this") reveals both name and origin of the master. The body is decorated with a multi-figured composition in relief portraying a hunt, evidently of some barbarian chief. There are traces of bright paint over the white ground.

59, 60. Mould and cast for the mask of Dionysos

Greece. 3rd century B.C.
Pottery. Height 19.8 cm
Received in 1888 (found in Chersonesus, near Sevastopol).
Inv. No. X 1888.43

The clay mould was made by a Chersonesus craftsman from a small Archaic marble head of Dionysos, found in the same place two years later. The mould could have been used for making coloured clay copies.

61. Playing Girls

Corinth. Late 4th–early 3rd century B.C.
Terra-cotta. Height 26 cm
Recieved in 1884 from the P. Saburov collection, St. Petersburg.
Inv. No. Г 577

Terra-cotta statuettes were made in many other artistic centres apart from the famous workshops of Tanagra. The group representing two playing girls, the loser carrying the winner on her back was made in Corinth.

62

62. Girl Standing

Tanagra. 3rd century B.C.
Terra-cotta. Height 18 cm
Received in 1884 from the P. Saburov collection, St. Petersburg.
Inv. No. Γ 445

This figurine is considered to be one of the most accomplished pieces of genre art practised by masters of Tanagra in Boetia. The familiar, everyday naturalism of terra-cottas serves as a perfect illustration of Greek women's way of life in the Classical period, as well as the kind of clothing and decorations they wore and their habits and pastime.

63

63. Ear-ring

Greece. First half of the 4th century B.C.
Gold, decorated with enamels. Length 9.5 cm
Received in 1831 (found in the Kul-Oba barrow near Kerch).
Inv. No. K-O 6

The ear-ring is an example of the so-called "microtechnique" for which the goldsmiths of Athens were especially noted in the 5th and 4th centuries B.C. The specimen consists of a richly ornamented disk and a crescent with pendants of an amphora shape hanging from it by fine chains. The joints are disguised by petalled rosettes of different size. The entire surface of the ear-ring is covered with an elaborate filigree design composed of festoons, volutes, and a variety of ornaments reproducing motifs of architectural decoration. Some of the details and the disk itself are bordered by tiny gold grains and encrusted with enamel. Around the large rosette are four smaller ones alternating with four minute sculptural groups of nereids riding dolphins. Each of the nereids carries a sword, a helmet, or some other piece of armour which, according to the legend, the goddess Thetis sent to her son Achilles.

64, 65 ▶

64, 65. Red-figure lecanis

Attica, Greece. 4th century B.C. The Eleusinian Painter
Pottery. Dia. 38.2 cm
Received in 1859 (found in the Yuz-Oba barrow near Kerch). Inv. No.
Ю-О 9

Flat vessels of this kind were used for keeping jewellery. Therefore their lids were often painted with scenes of the life in the Gynaeceum, the women's apartments in a house. The painted, often heightened with gilding, compositions on fourth-century red-figure vases show a marked influence of the mural paintings of the time.

66

66, 67. Intaglio: *The Gorgon Medusa*

Greece. 5th century B.C.
Chalcedony and gold. 2.9 × 2.3 cm
Received in 1860 (found in the Yuz-Oba barrow near Kerch).
Inv. No. Ю-О 6

The seal with Medusa must have guarded its owner
against any harm or an evil eye. The figure is executed
in accordance with the "Knielaufschema" of Archaic
art: the legs and feet in profile and the body full face.
The fantastical winged creature harmonizes beautifully with the oval bluish stone.

68, 69, 70

68. Intaglio: *Bather*

Greece. 4th century B.C.
Chalcedony and gold. 2.6 × 2 cm
Received in 1836 (found in the necropolis at Panticapaeum, Kerch).
Inv. No. П1834/35.4

The proportions of the beautiful nude body bring to mind the statues by Praxiteles. A similar subject is also encountered in the Attic red-figure vases. The skill of the cutter is evident from the detailed modelling, elegant contour, and clear lines.

69. Ring: *Athena*

Eastern Mediterranean. 3rd century B.C.
Gold, set with garnet. Height 3.8 cm
Received in 1838 (found in the necropolis at Panticapaeum, Kerch). Inv. No. П 1838.15

The massive ring, of rare size and shape, is adorned with a big garnet inset—the head of Athena in high relief.

70. Ring: *Seated Aphrodite and Cupid*

Greece. 4th century B.C.
Gold. Height 2.2 cm
Received in 1864 (found in the Bolshaya Bliznitsa barrow, Taman peninsula). Inv. No. ББ 38

The ring is adorned with a chased representation of Aphrodite playing with Cupid. It is distinguished for its exquisite silhouette, precision of line, and fine finish of detail. Such gold rings, in addition to cut gemstones, were used as seals.

71, 72, 73

71. Cameo: *Hera*

Rome. 1st century A.D.
Sardonyx. 2.9 × 2.2 cm
Provenance unknown. Inv. No. Ж 308

The cameo with the image of Hera is a fine specimen of the Classical art of the period of Augustus. The cold profile of Hera is clearly outlined, framed by the soft waves of the hair. This representation bears resemblance to numerous statues of the goddess.

72. Cameo: *The Judgement of Orestes*

Rome. 1st century B.C.
Sardonyx. 2.9 × 3.9 cm
Received in 1830 from the A. Vlasov collection. Inv. No. Ж 300

The subjects of multi-figured compositions may have been borrowed by the gem-carvers from the paintings of the Hellenistic period. The scene of the judgement of Orestes, who killed his mother in revenge for his father, is treated with an expressiveness rarely met in cameos.

73. Intaglio: *Sibyl*

Rome. 1st century B.C.–1st century A.D. By Hyllos
Cornelian. 2 × 1.6 cm
Received in 1925 from the Yusupov collection, St. Petersburg.
Inv. No. Ж 6656

The intaglio with the image of a sibyl was made by Hyllos, the famous engraver of the days of Augustus. He drew his subjects and images from Classical Greek art. The generalized forms match the exquisite finish of detail, which makes the gem especially ornate.

74. The Gonzaga Cameo

Alexandria. 3rd century B.C.
Sardonyx. 15.7 × 11.8 cm.
Received in 1814 from the Josephine de Beauharnais collection.
Inv. No. Ж 291

The Gonzaga cameo, so called after its first owners, the Gonzaga Dukes of Mantua in Italy, was produced in Alexandria by an unknown master. The rulers of Ancient Egypt, Pharaoh Ptolemy (II) Philadelphus and his wife Arsinoë, are portrayed in an idealized manner—as gods of the Greek Pantheon. The three basic layers of the stone—the upper, brown one, used for rendering the helmet, hair, and aegis of the king, the intermediate one, with its milky-bluish iridescence, retained for carving out the profiles of the royal couple, and the black of the background against which the faces stand out so clearly—are all exploited by the lapidary with a virtuosity that immediately strikes the eye. His particular subtlety in handling the stone reveals itself in moulding Arsinoë's features for which only a thin vein of white is taken, thus creating a powerful light-and-shade effect.
In passing from one collection to another the gem was seriously damaged and had to be restored.

96

74

75

75. Pendant: *Nereid Carrying Armour to Achilles*

Greece. 4th century B.C.
Gold. Height 12 cm
Received in 1864 (found in the Bolshaya Bliznitsa barrow, Taman peninsula).
Inv. No. ББ 31

The pendant is a part of the ceremonial head-dress of a Bosporan priestess of Demeter. The exact purpose of such pairs of pendants, found only in the burials of the Northern Black Sea Coast, is not known. They may have been attached to a diadem or worn as pectoral ornaments.

76. Vessel: *Scythian Warriors*

Greece. 4th century B.C.
Electrum. Height 13 cm
Received in 1831 (found in the Kul-Oba barrow near Kerch). Inv. No. K-O 11

This globular vessel is one of the most remarkable specimens of Greek metalwork found in the Northern Black Sea Coast region. Its body is chased with scenes derived from Scythian mythology, which makes the vessel a highly valuable source of information on Scythian life.

78

78. Harness ornament: *The Gorgon Medusa*

Mediterranean. 1st century B.C.
Silver-gilt. Diameter 17.5 cm
Received in 1906 (found in 1900 in the Akhtanizovka barrow, Taman peninsula). Inv. No. Ахт 18

The head of the Gorgon Medusa, embossed in high relief, seems to have had an apothropaeic meaning. It was probably meant to guard both horse and rider against evil. Such images were widespread in the metalwork of the Late Hellenistic period. But this particular ornament from Akhtanizovka is remarkable for its imposing forms and the expressiveness of the wonderfully modelled face.

77. Amphora

Alexandria. 1st century A.D.
Glass. Height 19.5 cm
Received in 1910 (found in the necropolis at Panticapaeum, Kerch).
Inv. No. П 1910.38

The amphora found at Panticapaeum is a rare specimen of Roman painted glass. The main centre of its production was in Alexandria, Egypt. This amphora may have also been produced there.

79. Portrait of a Man

Rome. Last quarter of the 1st century B.C.
Bronze. Height 39 cm
Recieved in 1928 from the State Museum Reserve. Inv. No. B 2067

The head of a Roman, probably a fragment of an equestrian statue, is a rare specimen of the Roman bronze sculpture preserved to our time. The strongly marked facial features are typical of the portraits of the Republic period, although the expression of sadness is unusual. The unshaven face was a sign of mourning with the Romans.

80. Portrait of a Syrian Woman

Rome. 160–180 A.D.
Marble. Height 30 cm
Received before 1850 (provenance unknown). Inv. No. A 583

The marble head, probably part of a funerary statue, is a true masterpiece of Roman sculpture. It reveals the rich inner world of the woman with a skill unusual for the time. The portrait may have been produced by a Greek sculptor; it is imbued with an elated poetical feeling rarely, if ever, observed in Roman sculptural portraits.

81

81. Scales weight: portrait of Caligula (?)

Rome. First half of the 1st century A.D.
Bronze. Height 16 cm
Received in 1846 (found in Pompeii?). Inv. No. B 61

The weight in the form of a portrait bust is executed with an unusual skill. The face of the future Emperor reveals a family likeness to Octavian Augustus.

82. Mask of Rhescuporis

Northern Black Sea Coast. 3rd century A.D.
Gold. Height 22 cm
Received in 1838 (found in the tomb of Rhescuporis, Kerch). Inv. No. P 1

The portrait mask of the Bosporan King Rhescuporis is a masterpiece of third-century goldwork. The gold sheet was first beaten over a mould, with subsequent finish by hand. This is the only known specimen of a funerary gold mask yielded so far by Bosporan graves.

83

84. Chariot decoration: *Triton*

Thrace. Late 2nd–early 3rd century A.D.
Bronze. Height 12.2 cm
Received in 1894 from the Academy of Sciences, St. Petersburg (found in 1878 in Bulgaria). Inv. No. B 866

The bronze sculptures from the set of funeral decorations of a Thracian chariot were found in the Dukhova Mogila barrow (Bulgaria) in 1878. The beauty of their silhouettes, their plastic expressiveness and vivid decorative details rank these figures among the best examples of small-scale Roman bronzes of the late second and early third centuries A.D.

83. Chariot decoration: *Silenus*

Thrace. Late 2nd–early 3rd century A.D.
Bronze. Height 12 cm
Received in 1894 from the Academy of Sciences, St. Petersburg (found in 1878 in Bulgaria). Inv. No. B 870

84

85. Portrait of Emperor Balbinus

Rome. Second quarter of the 3rd century A.D.
Marble. Height 72.5 cm
Received in 1852 from the I. and A. Laval collection. Inv. No. A 250

Caelius Calvinus Balbinus was in power for only ninety-nine days and left no considerable trace in history. But his portraits have become a kind of evidence of the time. They reflected the general confusion preceding the fall of the formerly powerful Roman Empire, the collapse of antique philosophy and its humanistic ideals. Among the preserved portraits of Balbinus the Hermitage marble is the most expressive.

86. Portrait of Philip the Arab

Rome. *Ca.* mid-3rd century A.D.
Marble. Height 70 cm
Received in 1787 from the Lyde Browne collection (found in the mid-eighteenth century in Rome). Inv. No. A 31

Born in the Roman provinces, Philip the Arab had gone all the way from a soldier to an emperor. The sculptor created the effigy of a warrior and an imperious ruler, revealing his contradictory nature and intense inner world.

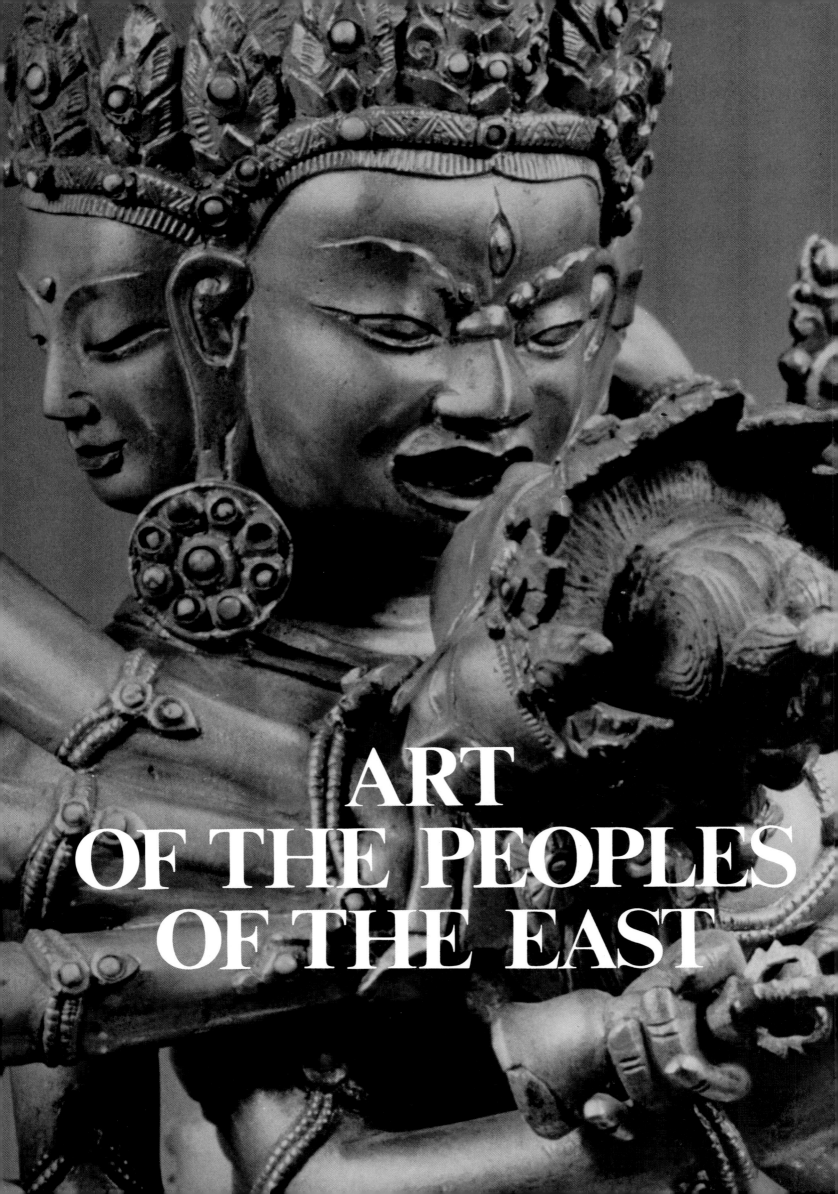

ART
OF THE PEOPLES
OF THE EAST

The Hermitage's Department of the Culture and Art of the Peoples of the East was set up in the autumn of 1920. Among those who played an active role in its organization were the distinguished Russian orientalists Nikolai Marr, Sergei Oldenburg, and Vasily Barthold. Appointed head of the department was their pupil Iosif Orbeli, whose indefatigable energy turned it into a veritable treasure-store of art monuments from the countries of the East. At the time of the department's inception the Hermitage already possessed a considerable number of items pertaining to Eastern art. Catherine II's eighteenth-century collection of glyptics, for example, contained not only antique gems, but also carved stones from Ancient Egypt, Mesopotamia, Iran, Byzantium, and China as well. Napoleon's Egyptian campaign and the great discovery of Jean-François Champollion, who was the first to decipher the hieroglyphics of Ancient Egypt in the early nineteenth century, aroused widespread interest in Egyptian art.

In 1826–27 the Academy of Sciences acquired the Castiglione collection and a number of carved wooden sarcophagi which were subsequently transferred to the Hermitage; later the Hermitage came into the possession of some magnificent samples of Egyptian sculpture, among them the statue of Sekhmet from the temple of Mut at Karnak (Luxor). The expeditions of Vladimir Bock to Egypt (1888–89 and 1897–98) enriched the Hermitage with Coptic fabrics, articles of bone and bronze, as well as pottery of the Arab period. Some works by masters of Eastern applied art entered the Museum in 1860 together with part of "Peter the Great's collection". In 1885 the collection of arms and armour thitherto housed in the Arsenal of Tsarskoye Selo (near St. Petersburg), and in 1910–11 the so-called Khiva treasure-trove, were transferred to the Hermitage. The acquisition of the well-known Basilewsky collection enriched the Museum with works of Byzantine art (ivory carvings, enamels, etc.).

During the nineteenth century Oriental relics entered the Hermitage together with material unearthed by archaeological expeditions on the territory of Russia. The discovery of Sassanian and Byzantine silverware in the Ural region in the 1880s is a case in point (the Hermitage collection of Sassanian silver numbers about 100 items and is considered one of the best in the world). Artifacts from North Caucasus burial sites excavated by Nikolai Veselovsky entered the Hermitage at the end of the century. The same Veselovsky also found, and in many cases bought, in Central Asia a significant number of unique bronzes. In the early years of the twentieth century Vasily Barthold began excavations at Afrasiab (ancient Samarkand), and all the material discovered there likewise entered the Hermitage.

All in all, by 1917 the Hermitage had already accumulated about 10,000 samples of Eastern art; working at the Museum were such outstanding orientalists as

Vladimir Golenishchev, Nikodim Kondakov, Yakov Smirnov, Alexander Markov, and others.

The creation of a separate Department of the East served as a powerful impetus for the growth of its collections. In the 1920s and 1930s collections from other museums and institutions were transferred to the Hermitage. Thus, in 1926 the Hermitage received from the museum of the former Stieglitz School of Art and Industrial Design its collections of applied art which included magnificent samples of Persian and Central Asian carpets, pottery, porcelain, and bronzeware. Another important addition was made in 1933–34, when the Ethnographic Department of the Russian Museum, Leningrad, ceded to the Hermitage materials excavated during the Mongolian and Szechwan expeditions of the well-known explorer and scientist Piotr Kozlov (1908 and 1926) who unearthed the Chinese city of Khara-Khoto (Iching). Destroyed in the thirteenth century by Genghis Khan's Mongol-Tartar armies, the city was buried by the sands of the surrounding desert. Discovered in the city itself and in the tomb of a Buddhist nun outside its walls were relics of artistic handicrafts, a unique collection of books and manuscripts in Chinese and Tangut, engravings and Buddhist icons of various schools. The Russian Museum also handed over relics from the Hun tumuli of the Noin-Ula mountains (Mongolia, 1926). Thanks to the permafrost the lacquers, wooden articles, and silks found there were in good condition. The silks made up the core of a collection of early Chinese fabrics (first centuries A.D.) which is today world-famous.

The Leningrad Museum of Ethnography and Anthropology of the USSR Academy of Sciences contributed the various Buddhist relics brought by Academician Sergei Oldenburg from expeditions to the northern oases of Sinkiang (1909–10) and the town of Tunhuang (1914–15).

The Russian Museum also handed over numerous Byzantine and Greek icons previously housed in the collections of Nikolai Likhachov and Piotr Sevastyanov. Likewise originating from the Likhachov collection is a magnificent library of cuneiform texts reflecting different aspects of the social, economic, and cultural life of some of the most ancient world civilizations (the earliest monuments date to the fourth millennium B.C.). The library boasts a wide variety of legal documents, mathematical tablets, literary works, and several world-famous Egyptian papyri, such as *The Tale of the Shipwrecked Sailor* and *The Prophecy of Neferti*. The relics of Byzantine sphragistics from the Likhachov collection and from the former Russian Archaeological Institute in Konstantinople are of enormous interest to students of Byzantine history.

Many artistic handicraft items were acquired in the village of Kubachi (North Daghestan) which has long been renowned not only for its skilful armourers, but also as a singular art reserve of rare mediaeval Eastern fabrics, carpets, bronzes, and pottery assembled by its inhabitants over the years.

In the 1930s the department organized a number of archaeological expeditions which yielded relics from some precisely dated complexes in Central Asia and the Caucasus. Quite a few of these expeditions continue their work to this day in cooperation with research institutes based in the relevant Soviet republics.

At the present time the Hermitage has in its possession about 160,000 items pertaining to the culture and art of various Eastern countries, of which 8,000 are on permanent display in seventy-three of the Museum's rooms.

Ancient Egypt is represented mainly by figurines, sculptures, handicraft items, and papyri. Although the exhibition does not reflect all the stages in the evolution of Egyptian art with due completeness, each period is nevertheless illustrated by some excellent relics (for example, a black granite statue of Amonemhet III or a wooden statuette of a young man).

The art of Asia Minor is represented by some top-quality samples of Assyrian and Achaemenid glyptics, reliefs from Palmyra, and the famous bilingual tariff discovered by the Russian traveller Semion Abamelek-Lazarev and brought to the Hermitage in 1902.

The sections of the exhibition devoted to the Caucasus and Central Asia cover a very long historical period—from the origin of class societies to the mid-nineteenth century. The Caucasian section features materials from Urartu, the most ancient state on the territory of the USSR. Many of these materials were excavated at Karmir-Blur (Red Hill, a former Urartu fortress) by Academician Boris Piotrovsky. They include such relics as feast bowls inscribed with the names of the country's rulers in the eighth century B.C., samples of small-size sculpture, and a variety of pottery. The collection also contains mediaeval bronzes, and in recent years it has been enriched by excellent mediaeval fabrics from the North Caucasian burial place of Moshchevaya Balka.

The Central Asian section, alongside such interesting items as a bronze altarpiece from the Semirechye area (fourth century B.C.), the famous Airtam frieze (first century A.D.), and murals from Pyanjikent and Varakhsha unearthed by Soviet archaeologists in Uzbekistan and Tadjikistan, also includes first-rate collections of glazed pottery, bronzes, patterned fabrics, and carpets of the late Middle Ages, eighteenth- and nineteenth-century side arms. The latest additions to the collection are samples of monumental painting and sculpture from the Buddhist monastery of Ajina-tepe in South Tadjikistan.

The exhibition devoted to the culture and art of Byzantium and the Near East has on display a world-famous collection of sixth- and seventh-century Byzantine silverware, beautiful objects of carved ivory, enamels, and one of the finest collections of twelfth- to fifteenth-century icons anywhere; the art of Sassanian Iran is represented by silver vessels, coins, and glyptics. An admirable collection of mediaeval Iranian bronzes reflects the evolution of this art over a thousand-year period (eighth to eighteenth century). Also on display are samples of Syrian glass, a rich collection of fifteenth- to nineteenth-century Persian and Turkish ceramics, Iranian carpets, miniatures, and oil paintings from the Qajar dynasty period.

The exhibition reflecting the art and culture of the Far East (China, Japan, India, Indonesia, Mongolia) includes materials from a famous cave monastery near the town of Tunhuang on China's western border, the so-called Cave of a Thousand Buddhas—icon fragments, murals, sixth- to tenth-century loess sculpture, a very rich collection of mediaeval Buddhist icons from Khara-Khoto, monumental painting from oasis temples in Sinkiang, Indian miniatures of the Mogul period, magnificent Tibetan lama icons in the *tanka* tradition, and samples of Gohua painting. Well represented is the applied art of China, India, and Japan—porcelain, enamels, ivories, and painted and carved lacquer articles.

Members of the Hermitage staff study the most diverse aspects of the art and culture of the East—the social and economic life of the ancient states of Mesopotamia, various problems of urban life in mediaeval times as reflected by materials from Pyanjikent and Khara-Khoto, cultural contacts between the East and the West from early times to the eighteenth and nineteenth centuries.

The Department of the East has established close contacts with foreign museums (for example, the Guimet Museum in Paris, or the Department of Antiquity of the Metropolitan Museum in New York).

Members of the department's research staff invariably take part in international congresses and symposiums on Eastern art and culture and help organize temporary exhibitions at the Hermitage and abroad.

Items from the department's extensive collection have been shown in Tokyo, London, Paris, Munich, and Berlin. There is an ongoing exchange of exhibitions between the department and many major world museums. In March 1979 the British Museum displayed its treasure of the Oxus in the Hermitage, the first such demonstration outside Great Britain. The hoard is a unique collection of jewellery discovered on the territory of ancient Bactria (the right bank of the Amu Darya River in Central Asia).

The samples of Oriental art included in the present exhibition have been selected from the Hermitage collections for their exceptional artistic merits. The art of ancient Iran is represented by magnificent gold neck ornaments and a bowl with panther-shaped handles (fourth century B.C.); ancient Central Asia, by a unique sacrificial altar from the Semirechye area; Sassanian Iran, by world-famous silver dishes; mediaeval Iran, by excellent bronzes. Chinese painting is represented by a masterful portrait of an official and his wife (sixteenth century), the only sample of the Ming dynasty painting in the Hermitage, etc.

We sincerely hope that the works included in this volume will find favour with art lovers and will awaken in them a desire to visit the Hermitage to see the Museum's entire Eastern collection for themselves.

Tatyana Arapova

87. Gift-bearers

Ajina-tepe, Central Asia. Second half of the 7th century
Painting on loess plaster. 95 × 62 cm
Received in 1964 (found during excavation work by the Tadjik
archaeological expedition). Inv. No. B-1666

A fragment of a mural discovered in the Buddhist temple at Ajina-tepe in South Tadjikistan. The mural adorned the wall of the passage in the main stupa of the temple. It is a part of the composition depicting the offering of gifts to saints.

88. Young Man and Girl on Horseback

Pyanjikent, Central Asia. 8th century
Painting on loess plaster. 113 × 95 cm
Received in 1956 (found during excavation work by the Tadjik
archaeological expedition). Inv. No. CA-14864

The fragment of a mural which decorated a private house; the subject seems to have been borrowed from some literary work. Represented are a girl with a maiden hairdo and a young man on horseback. They are evidently the main characters of some romantic adventure. The spear lying at the horses' feet shows that their lives are endangered.

89. Bodhisattva

Eastern Turkestan. 9th century
Size colours on loess plaster. 37 × 33 cm
Received in 1930 from the Museum of Anthropology and Ethnography of
the USSR Academy of Sciences, Leningrad (found by the second Turkestan expedition of S. Oldenburg in 1914–15). Inv. No. TУ-783

The type of a rounded youthful face with massive features was characteristic of the Uigur art school of the ninth century. According to iconographical rules, the Bodhisattva is wearing a magnificent crown and a rich
necklace. His hands are folded in the prayer and deference gesture.

90. Buddha Amida and Bodhisattvas Avalokiteshvara (Kuan Yin) and Mahastamaprabti Receiving the Soul of a Righteous Man into the Land of Bliss—Sukhavati

Khara-Khoto, China. 12th century
Mineral colours on silk. 113 × 60.5 cm
Received in 1933–34 from the Russian Museum, Leningrad (found by the
Mongol-Szechwan expedition of P. Kozlov in 1908–9). Inv. No. X-2415

The Bodhisattvas standing before the Buddha hold a lotus throne and are
ready to receive the soul, represented as a small baby. This is one of the
most common susbjects to be seen on the icons found in Khara-Khoto.

91. The Bodhisattva of Mercy, Kuan Yin

Khara-Khoto, China. 12th century
Mineral colours on silk. 125 × 56.5 cm
Received in 1933–34 from the Russian Museum, Leningrad (found by the
Mongol-Szechwan expedition of P. Kozlov in 1908–9). Inv. No. X-2434

The Kuan Yin cult was widely spread in the Tangut state Xcy-xcja. The
Bodhisattva is seated on a high throne. In his right hand he holds a *ju-i*
sceptre (symbolizing granting of the wishes). The Bodhisattva wears a
traditional robe and a crown with an image of Buddha Amida.

89

92. Deity of the Saturn Planet

Khara-Khoto, China. 12th century
Mineral colours on paper. 93.5 × 62 cm
Received in 1933–34 from the Russian Museum, Leningrad (found by the
Mongol-Szechwan expedition of P. Kozlov in 1908–9). Inv. No. X-2451

The personification of the deity as an old man plodding his way may be explained by the slow movement of the Saturn planet in the solar system.

93, 94. Kuan Yui

Khara-Khoto, China. 12th century
Woodcut. 71 × 33 cm
Received in 1933–34 from the Russian Museum, Leningrad (found by the
Mongol-Szechwan expedition of P. Kozlov in 1908–9). Inv. No. X-2519

General Kuan Yui, who lived in the third century, continued to be popular up to the twentieth century. He is represented sitting on a throne, surrounded by five warriors. On the banner is the character *kuan*, the family symbol of Kuan Yui. An inscription on the woodcut reads: "The Prince of Faith and Courage, fighting and peace-making" (the title bestowed upon Kuan Yui by the emperors of the Sung dynasty in the twelfth century). The text on the side of the woodcut says that it was executed by the master Sui in the town of P'ingyangfu, the most prominent centre of book-printing in China in the Sung epoch.

93

95. Buddha Shakyamuni with Bodhisattvas Fugen and Monju

Japan. 14th century
Mineral colours on silk, touched with gold. 120 × 67 cm
Received in 1973 through the Hermitage Purchasing Commission.
Inv. No. ЯТ-3455

The Buddha, flanked by the Bodhisattvas, is in the centre of the picture. Surrounding them are sixteen guardians and deities personifying various planets of the solar system.

96, 97. An Official and His Wife

China. 16th century
Mineral colours on silk. 144 × 106 cm
Received in 1971 from the N. Altman collection, Leningrad.
Inv. No. ЛТ-7548

A rare specimen of Chinese ritual portraiture connected with the cult of the ancestors. The man is dressed as an official of the fifth rank, wearing a head-dress—*pu tou*—and a red robe with puffed sleeves embroidered with birds. The wife is dressed accordingly, in a red robe with a long scarf round her shoulders—*pei tzŭ*.

98, 99. Yama, the Lord of Death

Tibet. 19th century
Gouache on linen. 145 × 98 cm
Received in 1967 through the Hermitage Purchasing Commission.
Inv. No. KO-1013

Yama, the Lord of Death, is surrounded by sinners who are subjected to various tortures. The *thang-ka* is an excellent example of the Tibetan style of painting. It presents a special interest because of a later addition in the centre: two Europeans wearing helmets and glasses and smoking cigars are being dragged by a demon into Hell. The addition must have been made in the early twentieth century and was apparently a Tibetan response to English military actions of 1903–5. To the best of our knowledge, this *thang-ka* is the only example of traditional Tibetan painting used as a sort of political poster.

98, 99 ▶

100

MIHR-ALI

100. Portrait of Fath-Ali Shah.
1813–14

Iran
Oil on canvas. 118 × 253 cm
Received in 1932 from the Gatchina Palace Museum
near Leningrad. Inv. No. УР-1108

This official portrait of Fath-Ali shah was executed by Mihr-Ali, one of the most prominent painters at his court. It is an excellent example of the so-called Qajar style, which is characterized, at its early stage, by a whole system of technical and iconographical rules, by strict regimentation of subjects and their treatment.

101. Woman with Flowers.
Mid-19th century

Iran
Oil on canvas. 89 × 153 cm
Received in 1928 through the Hermitage Purchasing
Commission. Inv. No. УР-1111

The dress, hairstyle, and ornaments are typical of the middle of the nineteenth century. By that time the manner of the Qajar style had considerably changed; there appeared a marked tendency to make the characters more true to life.

SHARAF AL-HUSAINI AL-YAZDI

102. Youth with a Lute. 1594–95

The Qazvin school, Iran
Miniature on paper. 20.4 × 29.4 cm
Received in 1924 from the Museum of the Stieglitz School of Art and
Industrial Design, Leningrad. Inv. No. УР-701

The pictorial treatment of the subject is typical of the art school which
existed in the second half of the sixteenth century in Qazvin, the second
capital of Safavid Iran. We know of no other works by this master.

104, 105. Man on Horseback and His Attendants. Second quarter of the 17th century

The Mogul school, India
Miniature on paper. 37 × 28 cm
Received in 1930 from Leningrad University. Inv. No. УП-961

The youth wears a magnificent robe. There is a green-and-gold halo round his head, which shows that he belongs to the ruling Mogul dynasty. He is accompanied by attendants who carry a peacock fan and the Sun emblem. The representation of the clouds in the picture reveals the influence of European art.

103. The Reposing Youth. Early 17th century

The Isfahan school, Iran
Miniature on paper. 20.3 × 31.3 cm
Received in 1924 from the Museum of the Stieglitz School of Art and Industrial Design, Leningrad. Inv. No. УР-706

The treatment of the subject of the miniature and the floral design of the background are typical of the art school which appeared at the beginning of the seventeenth century in Isfahan, the new capital of Safavid Iran.

106

106. Ladies on the Palace Terrace (Musicians).
17th century

The Mogul school, India
Miniature on paper. 15.5 × 7.8 cm
Received in 1930 from Leningrad University. Inv. No. УР-685

A scene from court life is probably depicted here: two young women sit on an open terrace; one plays the *vina* (a string instrument), the other the *tabla* (a small drum). The colours of the parterre, which can be seen beyond the balustrade of the terrace, echo in a subdued manner the bright greens and lilacs of their dresses.

107

107. Shiva and Parvati. 18th century

The Kangra school, India
Miniature on paper. 20.3 × 14.8 cm
Received in 1968 (gift of the Government of India). Inv. No. ИС-381

The family of Shiva is depicted at rest on the Kaylasa mountain, amid the
snow-capped peaks. Shiva himself, his consort Parvati, and their son, the
elephant-headed Ganesha, are seated comfortably on a tiger skin. Before
them stands Nandi, the sacred bull.

108

108. Head of the Buddha (?)

Ajina-tepe, Central Asia. Second half of the 7th century
Clay. 19 × 16 cm
Received in 1964 (found during excavation work by the Tadjik arch-
aeological expedition). Inv. No. B-1615

The hair is stamped into rows of curls and painted
blue. The head was found in the shrine of the Buddhist
monastery at Ajina-tepe.

109. Guhyapati

Tibet. 18th century
Gilt bronze. Height 24 cm
Received in 1934 from the Russian Museum, Leningrad (the Ukhtomsky
collection). Inv. No. У-1078

Guhyapati is one of the forms of Adi-Buddha (the
Supreme Buddha) Vajradhara. The *vajra* thunderbolt
and the prayer-bell *(ghanta)*, which Guhyapati holds
in his original hands, are both the attributes of Vajradhara. The bronze represents Guhyapati and his consort in a close embrace symbolizing the unity of the
cognitive, female, and the operational, male, elements.

148

**110. Siege of a Town by the Army
of Tiglatpalasar III (744–727 B.C.)**

Assyria
Limestone. 82 × 77 cm
Provenance unknown. Inv. No. 1834

The fragment of the relief from the palace of Tiglatpalasar III in Calah
(now Nimrud) represents bowmen protected by shield-bearers.

111

111. Altar

The Semirechye area, Central Asia. 4th century B.C.
Bronze. 125 × 122 cm
Received in 1930. Inv. No. CA-13760

The edge of the altar is decorated with sculptured figures of fantastic winged beasts resembling snow-leopards or tigers.

112. Bowl

Iran. 5th–4th century B.C.
Gold. Height 9.3 cm
Received in 1860 from the *Kunstkammer*, St. Petersburg (found near
Astrakhan). Inv. No. СИ-1727/71

The deep bowl with horizontal gadrooning is similar in shape to the vessels depicted in Persepolis reliefs. However, the handles shaped as beasts with arched backs and heads turned backwards which are roughly clenched to the body of the bowl are typical of Sakae art.

113. Necklace

East Iran. 5th–4th century B.C.
Gold, decorated in coloured enamels. Length 18 cm
Received in 1860 from the *Kunstkammer*, St. Petersburg (found near
Astrakhan). Inv. No. Z-568

The necklace (torque) is one of the best specimens of Achaemenid toreutics. It consists of two parts joined by a sleeve. Each of the two cast griffins decorating the ends of the torque is made of two halves subsequently soldered. The heads of the griffins were cast separately and joined to the bodies later.

112

113

114

114. Rhyton shaped as a ram's head

Iran. 5th–4th century B.C.
Silver. Length 22 cm
Received with the Siberian collection of Peter the Great (found before
1727). Inv. No. S-274

The shape of the rhyton is typical of objects belonging to Achaemenid
toreutics. In Iranian mythology the ram was a symbol of luck and well-
being.

115

115. Phalaros with warriors mounted on an elephant

Bactria (?). 3rd–2nd century B.C.
Silver-gilt. Diameter 24.7 cm
Received with the Siberian collection of Peter the Great (found before
1718). Inv. No. S-64

The representations of warriors are close to those of rulers with helmets on
their heads found on Graeco-Bactrian and Graeco-Indian coins of the
second and first centuries B.C.

116

116, 117. Dish with Shah-an-Shah

Iran. 7th century
Silver-gilt, with niello decoration. Diameter 24.8 cm
Received in the late 19th century by the Hermitage Archaeological Board
(found in 1878 near Perm in the Urals). Inv. No. S-13

On the basis of a number of iconographical (the Shah-an-Shah wears the so-called Sassanid crown) and technical peculiarities (the stripes on the tigers' skins are made by nielloing), the dish may be attributed to the early Islam period.

118

118. Dish with a lion and a doe

East Iran. 7th century
Silver-gilt. Diameter 27.2 cm
Received in the late 19th century by the Hermitage Archaeological Board
(found before 1880 near Perm in the Urals). Inv. No. S-23

The subject represents a late version of the vernal equinox, an ancient symbol of the Near East. Its iconography, the use of *repoussé* technique and some other details allow to attribute the dish to Sogdian craftsmen.

119. Dish with two fighting warriors

Central Asia. 7th century
Silver-gilt. Diameter 20.3 cm
Received in the late 19th century by the Hermitage Archaeological Board
(found in 1893 near Perm in the Urals). Inv. No. S-33

The composition is similar to the one discovered on a mural from Pyan-jikent. The warriors are fighting with swords, maces, and axes: broken weapons lie at their feet. To judge by the Pyanjikent mural, the warrior with a bow is to win in the fourth round.

120

120. Ewer

Iran. 8th–9th century
Bronze (brass). Height 25.7 cm
Received in 1925 from the A. Bobrinsky collection, Leningrad.
Inv. No. КЗ-5757

The massive cast ewer with a plant design belongs to a rare group of objects
produced in Iran during the first years of the Arab Caliphate.

121

121. Horse

Iran. 9th–10th century
Bronze. Length 42 cm
Received in 1925 from the A. Bobrinsky collection,
Leningrad. Inv. No. ИР-1984

The figure of the horse was used as a base
(probably of a lamp). There may have
been a rider originally. The entire surface
is covered with an engraved design; the
harness bears traces of an Arabic inscription reading: "Allah blesses thee."

122. Aquamanile

Iran. 7th–8th century
Bronze, inlaid with coloured paste. Length 34.5 cm
Received in 1925 from the A. Bobrinsky collection,
Leningrad. Inv. No. К3-5765

The aquamanile is cast in the shape of a
goat, the eyes inlaid with coloured paste.
Lack of ornamentation is characteristic
of Sassanian bronzeware.

122

123

123. Kettle

Khurasan, Iran. 12th century
Bronze, inlaid with copper. Height 18 cm
Received in 1925 from the A. Bobrinsky collection, Leningrad.
Inv. No. ИР-1443

The kettle, probably used in a bath-house, is richly decorated with a design of plants and birds. In the first and third bands are Arabic inscriptions of well-wishing. The design and form of the kettle are typical of twelfth-century Khurassanian bronzeware.

124. Jug

Central Asia. 12th–13th century
Bronze, inlaid with copper. Height 27.5 cm
Received in 1930 from the Museum of Asian Art, USSR Academy of Sciences, Leningrad. Inv. No. CA-12680

The jug is richly decorated with well-wishing inscriptions and representations of fantastic animals. The bronzeware with this kind of decor was probably made in Central Asia in the twelfth and early thirteenth centuries. It reveals a strong influence of Khurassanian bronzeware.

125. Dish

China. 14th century
Porcelain, painted in cobalt blue. Diameter 46 cm
Received in 1926 from the Museum of the Stieglitz School of Art and
Industrial Design, Leningrad. Inv. No. ЛК-374

Underglaze painting is combined with moulded relief. Four rows of flowers
on the rim represent four seasons of the year: the plum-blossom (*mei hua*)
symbolizes winter, the peony spring, the lotus summer, and the chrysanthe-
mum autumn. The representations in the centre are of well-wishing character: thus, the grapes denote success in every undertaking; the pumpkin
expresses wishing of progeny; the rock, of longevity. The dish belongs to
a small group of porcelain pieces produced in the second half of the
nineteenth century, on the border of two periods—Yuan (1279–1368) and
Ming (1368–1644).

126. Pharmacy jar with the State Emblem of Russia

China. Early 18th century
Porcelain, painted in colours. Height 19.5 cm
Received in 1926 from the Museum of the Stieglitz School of Art and Industrial Design, Leningrad. Inv. No. ЛИ-88

Pharmacy jars were commissioned by Peter the Great for the Moscow pharmacies, reorganized in 1710. It is painted in colours of the *famille-verte* colour scale. The two-headed eagle—the state emblem of Russia—is depicted as a fantastic bird; on the shield, instead of St. George slaying the Dragon, a subject alien to the Chinese craftsman, he chose to depict a plant design.

126

127

127. Jug

Central Asia. 11th century
Pottery, painted under a glaze. Height 22 cm
Received in 1926 from the Museum of the Stieglitz School of Art and Industrial Design, Leningrad. Inv. No. CA-13204

The jug is decorated with a wide band of geometric design combined with stylized representations of birds.

167

128. Plate

Japan. 17th century
Porcelain, painted in colours and mounted in gilt bronze. Diameter 22 cm
Received in 1926 from the Museum of the Stieglitz School of Art and
Industrial Design, Leningrad. Inv. No. ЯК-1528

The plate is decorated with a design of blossoming bamboo, a pine-tree,
peonies, and two birds. It is executed in the Kakiemon style (a term derived
from the name of the owners of kilns in Chindzen Province, not far from
the city of Arita). This style of porcelain painting, following the Chinese
tradition, is characterized by light brushstrokes and an asymmetric design.

129

129. Indian-ink box

Japan. 17th century
Wood, covered with gold lacquer and inlaid with silver, alloys, and gold.
23 × 20 cm
Received in 1926 from the Museum of the Stieglitz School of Art and
Industrial Design, Leningrad. Inv. No. ЯР-702

The lid of the box is decorated with a landscape depicting rocks, mountains
overgrown with pines, and peach-trees and peasants' huts on the beach of
the bay. In the central part are *kirins*, fantastic creatures bouncing on the
waves. This motif, borrowed from China became popular in Japanese art
from the early seventeenth century.

WESTERN
EUROPEAN
ART

The Department of Western European Art is one of the oldest in the Hermitage. The beginnings of its picture gallery go back to 1764 when the Berlin merchant Johann Ernest Gotzkowsky, in payment of his debt to the Russian treasury, consigned his art collection to St. Petersburg. Among its 225 pictures, mainly by Dutch and Flemish painters, were several masterpieces by Rembrandt, Steen, Jordaens, and Snyders, as well as a gem of the Hermitage collection— *Young Man with a Glove in His Hand* by Hals.

The Russian Empress Catherine II is known to have relied in her art-collecting on the advice of Russian ambassadors to the courts of Europe and of European scholars and writers. In Paris, the leading art market of the eighteenth century, her counsellors were the philosopher and critic Denis Diderot, the encyclopaedist Melchior Grimm, the sculptor Etienne Maurice Falconet, and Prince Dmitry Golitsyn, the Russian ambassador in France from 1762 to 1768. All this largely determined the exceptional wealth and variety of the Hermitage acquisitions of French painting.

Among the very first Paris purchases were such outstanding canvases as *Landscape with Polyphemus* by Poussin, *The Doctor's Visit* by Metsu, Murillo's *Rest on the Flight into Egypt*, and *The Return of the Prodigal Son* by Rembrandt, the great master's finest piece in the Hermitage collection.

The most important acquisitions were made in the 1760s and 1770s in Dresden, London, Rome, and Brussels. In 1768 Count Karl Cobenzl of Brussels sold his art collection to the Hermitage. This collection consisted of forty-six pictures by Dutch and Flemish painters, including several by Rubens, and about 4,500 drawings, which formed the core of the Hermitage collection of graphic art. The Cobenzl collection included drawings by Dutch, German, Italian, and French masters. The bulk of the collection, inasmuch as it stemmed from Brussels, consisted of works by Flemish artists, among them Rubens (over 30 sheets), Van Dyck, and Jordaens. The collection contained several rare sheets by early Italian masters and a significant number of sixteenth-century French pencil portraits.

The next year, 1769, saw the purchase of another major batch of drawings—over 1,000 works from the collection of Count Heinrich Brühl of Dresden. Fourteen large sketchbooks featured drawings by artists of various sixteenth- to eighteenth-century schools: the Venetian school (Veronese and Titian), the Dutch school (Rembrandt and Ostade), and the French school (Vouet and Poussin). But the principal value of the Brühl collection lay in its paintings—about 600 works of the Dutch and Flemish schools—which served as a solid basis for the Hermitage picture gallery's Dutch and Flemish sections of today.

Many of the works from the Brühl collection are masterpieces which deserve special mention—Rembrandt's *Portrait of a Scholar* and *Portrait of an Old Man in Red*, Terborch's *Arrival of a Letter*, Ruisdael's landscapes, Poussin's *Descent from the Cross*, Watteau's *An Embarrassing Proposal* and *Rest on the Flight into Egypt*, Tiepolo's *Maecenas Presenting the Liberal Arts to Emperor Augustus*, and Cranach's *Venus and Cupid.*

The Cobenzl, Brühl, and other collections brought to the Hermitage large numbers of excellent prints which in the eighteenth century were kept together with the paintings and drawings.

Lack of space does not permit us to dwell at length on all the acquisitions then made. We must name, however, the most important ones, above all the collection of Pierre Crozat, a well-known art connoisseur of his time. The transaction was made with his heirs in Paris in 1772 through Diderot and Golitsyn. With the Crozat collection, the Hermitage received some masterpieces of the Italian school—Raphael's *The Virgin with the Beardless St. Joseph*, Giorgione's *Judith*, Titian's *Danaë*, and Veronese's *Pietà*. Other schools were also brilliantly represented: suffice it to mention *Danaë* and *The Holy Family* by Rembrandt, *Bacchus* and *Portrait of a Lady in Waiting* by Rubens, works by Van Dyck, Jordaens, Lenain, Lorrain, Watteau, and Chardin.

Of great significance for the Hermitage picture gallery was the purchase in 1779 of the collection of Robert Walpole numbering 198 canvases—the largest private collection in England in the eighteenth century. Especially well represented in it both in scope and variety was Italian painting. The same applies to seventeenth-century Flemish painting, where mention should be made of Rubens' *Feast at Simon the Pharisee's*, *The Carters*, and a series of sketches for triumphal arches, several Van Dyck portraits of his English period, Snyders' *Bird Concert* and his four-picture *Shop* series. Aside from a few additions made later this important acquisition virtually completed the formation of the Hermitage picture gallery's Flemish collection.

The last major acquisition in the eighteenth century was the purchase in Paris of the Count Baudouin collection of 119 canvases, which included nine excellent paintings by Rembrandt.

Apart from large collections, individual works were purchased from some of the foremost eighteenth-century artists—Greuze, Chardin, Van Loo, Reynolds, and bought at auctions in Paris and Holland.

By the late 1700s the pictures hung in the galleries of the Small Hermitage and in several halls of the Winter Palace had come to cover the walls from floor to ceiling. The works were arranged not according to schools or periods, but mainly on the decorative principle (which, incidentally, was true of most European picture galleries of the time). No visitors were admitted, the only exceptions being a few art lovers, foreigners, and teachers and students from the St. Petersburg Academy of Arts. Lord Chamberlain K. Naryshkin's apt phrase to the effect that "the Hermitage is not a public museum, but a continuation of the Imperial Palace" well illustrated the actual state of affairs which was to last until the mid-nineteenth century.

Among the nineteenth-century acquisitions two, both made by Alexander I in 1814, were important—the purchase of thirty-eight pictures (including Rembrandt's *Descent from the Cross*) from the Malmaison palace of Empress Josephine, Napoleon's first wife; and about seventy Spanish canvases from the collection of the English banker Coesevelt, including works by Velázquez (*Count Duke of Oli-*

vares), Zurbarán (*The Girlhood of the Madonna*), and others. Together with Ribera's *St. Jerome* and Ribalta's *Three Saints in a Dungeon*, purchased in 1834 from Paez de la Cadeña, the Spanish ambassador in St. Petersburg, they formed the nucleus of the Hermitage's Spanish collection.

In the second half of the nineteenth century new acquisitions of painting and graphic art, while not ceasing altogether, were few. Purchased in 1910 from the well-known geographer and explorer Piotr Semionov-Tienshansky was a collection of Dutch and Flemish painting. In 1914 the Hermitage acquired Leonardo da Vinci's *Madonna with a Flower (The Benois Madonna)*, one of the Museum's most treasured gems.

The formation of the Hermitage's collection of Western European sculpture proceeded simultaneously with the acquisition of paintings for its picture gallery. Purchased in that period were works by such outstanding masters of different schools and epochs as Michelangelo, Falconet, Goudon, Canova, and a number of other eminent European sculptors.

The beginnings of the applied art collection with its porcelain, faience, fabrics, tapestry, silverware, and coloured stone sections go back to Peter the Great's time, when all these articles were widely used in the royal household, in palaces, and suburban residences. Acquisitions and donations continued to enter the Museum throughout the eighteenth and nineteenth centuries. One vitally important acquisition was the purchase in Paris in 1884 of the Basilewsky collection. This entry enriched the Hermitage collection, which had thitherto consisted of seventeenth- and eighteenth-century pieces, with numerous samples of mediaeval and Renaissance applied art: bone carvings, Limoges enamels, metalware, Italian majolica, French faience, and Venetian glass.

A significant enlargement of the Hermitage's stocks took place after the October Revolution of 1917 with the transfer to the Museum of nationalized collections of painting, graphics, and applied art from the Stroganov, Marble, and Yusupov palaces, the Academy of Arts museum, the museum of the Stieglitz School of Art and Industrial Design, and others.

In 1948 the Museum of Modern Western Art in Moscow gave the Hermitage 316 pictures by late nineteenth- and early twentieth-century artists. These had been acquired in the early 1900s by Moscow art collectors Sergei Shchukin and Ivan Morozov and included canvases by most of the major Impressionist and Post-Impressionist masters—Renoir, Monet, Cézanne, Gauguin, Van Gogh, Matisse, Picasso, Bonnard, Derain, and many others.

The augmentation of the Western European department's collections continues in our time as well. Several acquisitions have been made through the Hermitage's Purchasing Commission and at various exhibitions, many canvases have been presented to the Museum by artists and collectors. The past few years alone have seen the entry of pictures by Bellange, Teniers, Goya, Friedrich, Dufy, Boudin, and Matisse, graphic sheets by Cambiaso, Robert, Toulouse-Lautrec, Signac, Matisse, Picasso, Fougeron, and Richter.

At the present time the exhibition of the department is subdivided into sections devoted to the art of Italy, Spain, France, Holland, Flanders, Germany, and England. Rubens, Van Dyck, Poussin, Greuze, and Robert, who are very well represented in the collection, each have a separate room. A special section is devoted to Western European art of the nineteenth and twentieth centuries.

With but a few exceptions the painting, sculpture, and various fields of applied art of a particular country are exhibited together. Some rooms, however, contain only exhibits of the minor arts—silverware, porcelain, or carved stones. A whole suite of rooms, for example, is dedicated to the decorative arts of France.

The Department of Western European Art has loaned exhibits to almost all important international shows. Special exhibitions of paintings, drawings, and samples of decorative arts have been organized in a number of major world museums. Thus, Western European master drawings from the Hermitage have in recent years visited Dresden, Berlin, Prague, Budapest, Manchester, Vienna, Paris, Brussels, Sydney, Adelaide, and others.

In addition to demonstrating its own works of art, each year the department houses from ten to fifteen loan exhibitions. Among the most successful exhibitions from foreign museums held in the Hermitage were those from the Louvre and other French museums, from the New York Metropolitan Museum of Art, from the Dresden Picture Gallery, and many others.

The Hermitage has cultural contacts with an ever-increasing number of countries. Artistic exchanges, due to long-range planning, have become quite regular, especially with the twin cities of Leningrad—Dresden, Manchester, Milan, Rotterdam, Antwerp, and Le Havre.

Irina Novosselskaya

SIMONE MARTINI (SIMONE DI MARTINI).
Ca. 1284–1344
Italian school

130. The Madonna of the Annunciation. 1339–42

Tempera on panel. 30.5 × 21.5 cm
Received in 1911 at Count G. Stroganov's bequest from his collection in
Rome. Inv. No. 284
Right wing of a diptych. The left wing is presumed to have been the
Archangel, now in the National Gallery of Art, Washington

The Madonna of the Hermitage is a slightly altered replica of the figure of
Mary from the *Annunciation* dated 1333 (now in the Uffizzi, Florence).
Certain stylistic features suggest that the Hermitage picture may be dated
to Simone's late period, i.e. the time when he stayed in Avignon. It fully
epitomizes all that is characteristic of Martini's art—an enchanting beauty
and spirituality of the visual imagery, and an exquisite cadence of the
flowing, graceful linear design.

FRANCESCO PESELLINO (FRANCESCO DI STEFANO). 1422–1457
Italian school

131. An Allegory of Rome

Gouache and gold on parchment; borders in black pen, watercolours, and
gold. 28.7 × 20.2 cm (cut irregularly on edges)
Received in 1791 from Venice. Inv. No. 51

The Hermitage collection boasts of the six out of seven miniatures which
once illuminated the codex *De Secundo Bello Punico Poema* by Silius
Italicus. The seventh illumination is still in the codex, which is now in the
Biblioteca Marciana, Venice. The codex was said to have been commissioned by Pope Nicholas V, as shown by his portrait in one of the Hermitage
sheets. According to Giorgio Vasari, whose detailed description of these
excellent works was included in his story of Fra Angelico, the miniatures
were produced by the illuminator Attavante (1452–before 1517). However,
the miniatures are apparently of a much earlier date, revealing, as they are,
a great similarity to works by Francesco Pesellino, another Florentine
artist, a younger contemporary of Fra Filippo Lippi with whom he often
collaborated. The sheets from Silius Italicus' codex can evidently be as-
signed to the last years of Pesellino's short life, the period of flourishing of
his art.
The graceful figure of a young woman, depicted here holding an orb and
sceptre in her hands (symbolizing the victorious Rome), stands out in crisp
outlines against the background of sea and sky. The manner in which the
artist combines the monumental quality and grandeur of the woman's pose,
and the swift and impetuous movement of her body is really striking. The
pure, resonant tones of pigments, their original brightness so admirably
preserved, lend this sheet an unusual charm.

131

132

FILIPPINO LIPPI. *Ca.* 1457–1504

Italian school

132. The Adoration of the Infant Christ.
Mid-1480s

Oil on copper (transferred from panel). Tondo, dia. 53 cm
Received in 1911 from the Count P. Stroganov collection, St. Petersburg.
Inv. No. 287

In Italy, from the second half of the fourteenth century onwards, the theme of the Nativity was frequently treated as that of the adoration of the Christ Child. The tondo of Filippino Lippi exemplifies the composition of that kind. The action is set in Paradise with its boundary symbolically marked off by a marble balustrade. The Infant Christ is under the protection of attendant angels. This picture testifies to a considerable progress made in depicting the landscape by the Florentine painters of the late fifteenth century. Not only is the aerial perspective skilfully rendered by the artist, but there is also a certain feeling of festivity pervading the whole composition which greatly adds to the mood of lofty solemnity of the moment described.

179

RAPHAEL (RAFFAELLO SANTI). 1483–1520

Italian school

133. The Madonna and Child (The Conestabile Madonna).
Late 1502 or early 1503

Tempera on canvas (transferred from panel). 17.5 × 18 cm
Received in 1881. Formerly, the Winter Palace collection, St. Petersburg.
Inv. No. 252

The Conestabile Madonna is one of Raphael's earliest works. The picture bears the mark of Perugino, Raphael's teacher, whose drawing *The Madonna and Child Holding a Pomegranate in His Hand* may have suggested its composition. This was corroborated in 1881 when, during the transfer of the painting from panel to canvas, it was discovered that Raphael had originally depicted the Virgin with a pomegranate in her hand, but subsequently had replaced it with a book. This minor change in the motif has not affected the overall concept of the work.

The picture has the circular form of the tondo, which required of the artist a superlative skill in integrating the composition. Raphael coped with the task brilliantly. The picture shows a perfect marriage of form and colour: the circular resiliency of its outer shape goes well with the soft curving contours of the mantle covering the Virgin's head and shoulders.

The traditional theme is here treated in a simple and poetic way. The image of the Madonna, so pure and delicate, is echoed in the freshness of a spring landscape.

Before its transfer onto canvas, the wooden base and its gilt frame, which was apparently made after a drawing by Raphael, constituted a harmonious whole. The painter's filigree brushwork is perfectly set off by the frame's intricate arabesque.

The painting still retains the typical Quattrocento tendency to the narrative —details of the landscape, such as a boat sailing on the lake or houses along the shore, are rendered by the painter with a painstaking care. Yet, even in this early work with its crystal clarity of visual imagery and figure arrangement and the beauty of the ouline, one can foresee the future founder of the monumental style of the Roman school of painting.

133

LEONARDO DA VINCI. 1452–1519
Italian school

134, 135. The Madonna and Child (The Litta Madonna)

Oil on canvas (transferred from panel). 42 × 33 cm
Received in 1865 from the Duke A. Litta collection, Milan. Inv. No. 249

Although began at a much earlier date—probably at the same time as *The Benois Madonna*—this picture was completed only around 1491 (it is by that year that Leonardo's signed drawing of a female head, now in the Louvre, is dated).

Owing to its superb figure arrangement, the painting enjoyed a tremendous popularity, so great, in fact, that a variety of copies made from it by Leonardo's contemporaries are now fairly well-known (they can be found in the world's major museums—in the Louvre, in the Museo Poldi-Pezzoli, Milan, in the National Gallery, London, and elsewhere).

134, 135

LEONARDO DA VINCI. 1452–1519
Italian school

136. The Madonna with a Flower (The Benois Madonna)

Oil on canvas (transferred from panel). 49.5 × 31.5 cm
Received in 1914 from the M. Benois collection, Petrograd. Inv. No. 2773

The Benois Madonna, one of the few undisputed works by the master, dates from 1478—a comparatively early period in his artistic career. We know this from a note made in Leonardo's own hand on a sheet of his *Notes and Drawings,* now in the Uffizzi, Florence.

Leonardo painted religious scenes in the genre style which was so characteristic of Quattrocento art. The young Mary, jovial and dressed up, is holding out a flower towards her infant. The flower, the four petals of which symbolize the Crucifixion, is endowed with yet another, deeper significance in the picture, namely the cognition of the world which begins with an infant's first unsteady movements.

The delicate treatment of light and shade gives the figures an almost palpable existence. Leonardo's innovative style did not go unnoticed by his contemporaries. In his book *The Treasures of Florence,* which came out in 1591, Francesco Bocchi wrote: "A wood panel painted in oil by Leonardo's hand is excellent in its beauty. It depicts Our Lady in a most ingenuous and painstaking manner. The figure of the Infant Christ is marvellous, his upturned face is incomparable in the depth of meaning and the consummate mastery of its execution."

136

MICHELANGELO BUONARROTI. 1475–1564
Italy

137. The Crouching Boy. *Ca.* 1524

Marble. Height 54 cm
Received in 1785 from the Lyde Browne collection, London. Inv. No. H. ск. 154

In the British Museum in London there is a sketch of one of the draft plans for the Medici Chapel showing two figures which are similar in pose to *The Crouching Boy*. Those statues were meant to be placed in niches so as to present the side view. One may conclude from this that the Hermitage statue was included in the overall design of the Medici Chapel and therefore should be dated around 1524. Some experts maintained that the work on *The Crouching Boy* was entrusted to one of Michelangelo's pupils—either to Pierino da Vinci or to Tribolo. This, however, seems unlikely as the high artistic merits of the statue point unambiguously to Michelangelo himseif as its author, although he may possibly have availed himself of the help of his assistants.

The general concept behind the work is not quite fully clarified. Some consider it the symbol of a soul unborn, others the genius of death. The image created by the sculptor goes surely far beyond the narrow scope of these interpretations, for it is, first and foremost, a tragic image personifying the man bowed down by some evil force, suffering both physically and spiritually. Observed in that light, the resemblance of *The Crouching Boy* to the other statues of the Medici Chapel becomes apparent.

138

ANTONIO ROSSELINO. 1427–1478
Italy

138. The Madonna and Child. 1460s

Marble. 67 × 54 cm
Received in 1915 from the A. Zhuravliov collection, Petrograd.
Inv. No. Н. ск. 517

Antonio Rosselino, along with Desiderio da Setti-
gnano, was the foremost Florentine sculptor of the
mid-fifteenth century. The Hermitage relief is a superb
example of Rosselino's painterly manner. The theme
had repeatedly attracted the sculptor but rarely did he
attain such eloquence and freedom of design as in this
panel. That this was a fairly popular work in the
fifteenth century is amply evidenced by the existence
of numerous copies done in terra-cotta and plaster.

GIORGIONE (GIORGIO DA CASTEL-FRANCO). *Ca.* 1478–1510
Italian school

139. Judith

Oil on canvas (transferred from panel). 144 × 66.5 cm
Received in 1772 from the P. Crozat collection, Paris. Inv. No. 95

One of the few extant works by Giorgione, this picture
had, until the late nineteenth century, been ascribed to
Raphael.
During restoration work it was discovered that the
panel from which the painting was transferred onto
canvas had traces of door-hinges and a keyhole on it.
A conclusion was, therefore, made that originally the
picture had served as the door of a wall cupboard.

PAOLO VERONESE (PAOLO CAGLIARI). 1528–1588
Italian school

140. Pietà. Between 1576 and 1582

Oil on canvas. 147 × 111.5 cm (added strips on the left and on top)
Received in 1772 from the P. Crozat collection, Paris. Inv. No. 49

Pietà is one of the most recurrent themes in Venetian painting. Veronese, too, frequently turned to the subject, bringing it with the Hermitage canvas to unprecedented heights of pithiness and perspicuity.
The picture is notable for its superbly integrated composition: the interlocked hands of Christ and the angel tie it, as it were, in the foreground, the draperies beneath serve as the group's base, while the figure of Mary inclined towards Christ completes it from above. By juxtaposing cool greys of the dead Christ's body and pinks of the angel's garment the artist manages to create a colouristic effect of high emotional intensity which greatly adds to the overall dramatic content of the picture.

TINTORETTO (JACOPO ROBUSTI). 1518–1594
Italian school

141. Birth of St. John the Baptist. 1550s

Oil on canvas. 181 × 266 cm
Received in 1772 from the P. Crozat collection, Paris. Inv. No. 17

Dealing with a fairly obscure subject, the painter resolves it as a genre scene. As always with Tintoretto, his art here is a harmonious blend of the attainments in the use of colour made by Venetian artists and the narrative fluency of his own precise and highly imaginative manner.
A similarly entitled painting in the Venetian church of San Zaccaria is compositionally akin to the Hermitage canvas. It repeats, with minor alterations, the central group of women engaged in bathing the newborn baby. The Hermitage picture, however, is marked by a higher degree of technical perfection.

TITIAN (TIZIANO VECELLIO). 1485/90–1576
Italian school

142. St. Sebastian. *Ca.* 1570

Oil on canvas. 210 × 115 cm
Received in 1850 from the Barbarigo collection, Venice. Inv. No. 191

This picture was painted shortly before Titian's death. The figure of the martyr is lit by the flickering flames of a smoky fire obliterating the clear-cut outlines of objects in the background. The artist seems to be moulding form in colour, shaping it out of a single coherent mass of colouring matter in which no individual tones can be discerned. To his contemporaies such technique appeared so novel that Titian's late works executed in this manner were generally regarded as unfinished.

Titian's first intention was to paint a half-figure. Later, as the work progressed, the artist changed his mind and depicted the martyr full-length. The canvas had, therefore, to be lengthened, the added piece being of an entirely different type of weaving. As a result, the upper portion of the painting seems to have been brought to a higher degree of completion than its lower part where the toes and sandals of the man were only slightly outlined.

Titian himself must have looked upon the picture as a model as it never left his workshop during the artist's lifetime. He made its replica, though, of which we know only through Ridolfi's reference (1648) and a description by Abbé Ponçe (1788), who apparently saw it in the Escorial. Thus, the *St. Sebastian* of the Hermitage is not the only version of the picture as presumed before.

PONTORMO (JACOPO CARRUCCI).
1494–1556/7
Italian school

144. The Madonna and Child with St. Joseph and St. John the Baptist. Late 1551–early 1552

Oil on canvas. 120 × 98.5 cm (on both sides of the main picture are additional strips of canvas with the figures of St. Joseph and St. John the Baptist painted by the author)
Received in 1923 through the State Museum Reserve from the E. Mordvinova collection, Petrograd. Inv. No. 5527

The painting by Pontormo is a graphic illustration of Mannerism, a new painterly style evolved in the 1520s as a break-away trend shifting the accent from the ideals of harmonious beauty and naturalism of the High Renaissance towards the search for sharper contrasts, deeper expressiveness, and more heightened emotionalism.
By clashing the colours of his palette, by juxtaposing Mary's serenity and an agitated state of the Child, and through certain inconsistencies of the spatial arrangement of figures the artist manages to impart the composition a sense of anxiety alien to Renaissance art.

ANNIBALE CARRACCI. 1560–1609
Italian school

143. The Three Marys at the Tomb. Mid-1590s

Oil on canvas. 121 × 145.5 cm
Received from the W. Coesvelt collection, London. Inv. No. 92

This work was well known to the artist's contemporaries. The story of the picture's meanderings from collection to collection has reached us from different sources. The painting was executed for Signor Pasqualino from whom it passed to Cardinal Giovanni Battista Agucchi. Following the death of the latter it entered the collection of Cardinal Ascanio Filomarino. In the eighteenth century it was housed in the Palazzo of the Duke della Torre in Naples, and in the early 1800s it belonged to Lucien Bonaparte.

144

CARAVAGGIO (MICHELANGELO MERISI DA CARAVAGGIO). 1573–1610

Italian school

145. The Lute Player. *Ca.* 1595

Oil on canvas. 94 × 119 cm
Received in 1808 from the Giustiniani collection,
Paris. Inv. No. 45

This picture was painted for Cardinal Francesco Maria del Monte in whose house Caravaggio was living at the time. The artist himself considered this painting the best of all he had created.

In the nineteenth century the work was regarded as an allegory of love. Modern scholars seek to establish the affinity of its composition with the lyric poetry prevalent in the artist's time, seeing in it an eloquent expression of the ideals of universal love and harmony. It is in this vein that one can interpret the beginning of the madrigal by Jacques Arcadelt reproduced in one of the music-books: "Voi sapete ch'io v'amo" ("You know that I love you").

200

145

146

147

FRANCESCO GUARDI. 1712–1793

Italian school

146. Triumphal Arch on an Embankment

Pen and brown wash touched with watercolour and heightened with white
on paper. 28 × 19.1 cm.
Received in 1923 from the library of the former Stieglitz
School of Art and Industrial Design, Petrograd. Inv. No. 40787

This composition, with slight alterations, was frequently used by Guardi in his other drawings.
In style and subject-matter the Hermitage sketch belongs to the *capricci*, on which the artist worked in the 1770s and '80s.
According to Mikhail Dobroklonsky, the retouching of the sky with watercolour was probably done by another hand.

GIOVANNI BATTISTA TIEPOLO. 1696–1770

Italian school

147. Maecenas Presenting the Liberal Arts to Emperor Augustus. 1743

Oil on canvas. 69.5 × 89 cm
Received in 1769 from the Count H. Brühl collection, Dresden. Inv. No. 4

The picture was commissioned in 1743 by Count Algarotti for Count Heinrich Brühl, a minister of Augustus III, Elector of Saxony and King of Poland, and a great art lover and connoisseur whose position at the king's court may well be compared to that of Gaius Cilnius Maecenas, the trusted councillor of Emperor Augustus.
The three kneeling women personify the arts—painting, sculpture, and architecture—while the blind Homer is an embodiment of poetry. Tiepolo was unrivalled in rendering the intricate drapery of colourful garments and the space suffused with light and air.

203

148

ROGIER VAN DER WEYDEN (ROGIER DE LA PASTURE).
Ca. 1400–1464
Netherlandish school

148. St. Luke Painting the Virgin

Oil on canvas (transferred from panel). 102.5 × 108.5 cm
Received (the right-hand part representing St. Luke) in 1850 from the William III collection, the Hague, and in 1884 (the left-hand part representing the Madonna) from the art-dealer A. Baer, St. Petersburg. Inv. No. 419

The Apostle Luke is believed to be the patron-saint of artists. The subject of the present picture is borrowed from the apocryphal legend about St. Luke painting a miraculous portrait of the Virgin when she appeared to him in a vision. The features of the saint may possibly bear a resemblance to the artist himself.

The painting must have been very famous in its day, for several versions are extant, the best of which are to be found in Munich and Boston museums.

Like the majority of Netherlandish artists, Rogier van der Weyden worked in oils, using the techniques said to have been introduced by Jan van Eyck. He uses bright vibrant colours to reproduce the resplendence of the fabric and the golden embroidery.

205

ROBERT CAMPIN. *Ca.* 1380–1444
Netherlandish school

149. The Madonna and Child at the Fireside
(part of a triptych). 1430s

Oil on panel. 34.3 × 24.5 cm
Received in 1845 from the D. Tatishchev collection, St. Petersburg.
Inv. No. 442

Robert Campin, a major figure in Netherlandish art of the early fifteenth century, was for a long time known as the Master of Flemalle. Along with Jan van Eyck, Campin is regarded as the founder of fifteenth-century Netherlandish painting.

The panel gives a fair idea of the realist aspirations of the artist: in the scene depicted the spectator is offered a glimpse of the interior of a fifteenth-century Netherlands burgher's home. Such down-to-earth treatment of a religious subject lends the scene a vivid, lively atmosphere of a commonplace motif.

149

ROELANT JACOBSZ SAVERY. 1576–1639
Flemish school

150. The Country Fair (Peasant Holiday)

Watercolour and gouache over black chalk, in places touched with gold, on paper. 48 × 75.6 cm
Signed and dated, bottom centre: *Roeland Savery fec 1606*
Received in 1768 from the K. Cobenzl collection, Brussels. Inv. No. 5578

One of the most important drawings by Savery, *The Country Fair* was produced during the first years of the master's stay in Prague, at the court of Rudolph II. The high viewpoint and the motley character of the scenes depicted, as well as the true democratic spirit of the age-old Netherlandish traditions are all elements descending from the art of Pieter Breughel the Elder ("The Peasant Breughel").

This drawing, signed and dated by the artist, is of particular importance today as it sheds a new light upon the problem of identifying the author of a famous series of drawings *Naer het leven* (*From Life*) which until now were traditionally ascribed to the hand of Pieter Breughel the Elder. However, the fact that the two horses in harness depicted in the Hermitage sheet are an exact replica of the study in the series

mentioned above (Albertina, Vienna, Inv. No. 7867), and also the similar evidence of several figures in the foreground, give sufficient ground for attributing this whole series to Roelant Savery.

Unfortunately, very few drawings of such a format, executed in what was then called the "colour with water" technique, have come down to us. The reason for this should be sought in a poor resistance of this particular medium to ravages of time and atmosphere. This, on the other hand, makes the few extant works now found in major museums all the more valuable.

JAN VAN HUYSUM. 1682–1719
Dutch school

151. Bowl of Flowers

On the reverse: sketch of a vase of flowers
Red chalk and grey wash on paper. 46 × 32.4 cm
Received in 1923 from the library of the former Stieglitz School of Art and Industrial Design, Petrograd. Inv. No. 28575

Unlike his finished works, this compositional sketch by Van Huysum is done in a broad painterly manner.

151

REMBRANDT HARMENSZ VAN RIJN.
1606–1669
Dutch school

152. Danaë. 1636.
Repainted by the artist in 1646–47

Oil on canvas. 185 × 202.5 cm
Received in 1772 from the P. Crozat collection, Paris. Inv. No. 723

Danaë is one of the most significant works of the great
Dutch master. For over a hundred and fifty years the
painting remained the subject of an acute debate in the
scholarly circles as neither the subject nor the identity
of the model were established with sufficient certainty.
The new evidence, however, accumulated in the recent
years through a thorough investigation of a comprehensive documentary material and an X-ray study of
the picture has revealed unequivocally that about ten
years after the painting had been completed Rembrandt substantially repainted it. He altered the model's features, which had originally borne a strong likeness to the artist's early-departed wife Saskia, so as to
make them resemble those of Geertge Dircx. The
research has also confirmed that the subject of the
picture was based on the story of Danaë.

REMBRAND HARMENSZ VAN RIJN. 1606–1669
Dutch school

153, 154. The Return of the Prodigal Son. *Ca.* 1668

Oil on canvas. 262 × 205 cm
Signed, bottom left: *R f Rynf*
Received in 1776 through the mediation of D. Golitsyn from the d'Amesu-
ne collection, Paris. Inv. No. 742

This is the work in which the idea of love and compassion to the destitute
and suffering finds its supreme expression. Not only deeply humanitarian
in its message, but also perfect in its artistic idiom, both austere and subtle
at the same time, the picture stands as a magnificent culmination of Rembrandt's creative powers. More than that, it is justly regarded as one of the
greatest masterpieces of world art. The theme of love and forgiveness, as
embodied in the story of the prodigal son, was of lasting interest to
Rembrandt. He returned to it time and again in his etchings and drawings.
Yet, only in the Hermitage painting Rembrandt's visual imagery attains
such a degree of generalization that his portrayal of concrete motifs ac-
quires a universal value.

153, 154 ▶

155

PIETER DE HOOCH. 1629–after 1684
Dutch school

155. Mistress and Maid. *Ca.* 1657–58

Oil on canvas. 53 × 42 cm
Received in 1810 from the antiquary Lafontaine, Paris. Inv. No. 943

Pieter de Hooch, an outstanding master of Dutch genre painting, dedicated his entire career to depicting the unhurried life of the well-to-do Dutch bourgeois, shut away within a little world of his own—a house, a backyard, and a garden—where the troubles and worries of the real world outside could not reach him. The seventeenth-century town of Delft, where the picture was painted, was notable for its especially quiet and sedate tenor of life. The bright golden light suffusing the entire space of the painting emphasizes the impression of an immaculate tidiness of the place, imparting the scene the mood of placid tranquility and the sense of contended well-being.

The Hermitage canvas dates from the period when the artist was at the peak of his creative powers.

156

FRANS HALS. 1581/85–1666
Dutch school

156. Young Man with a Glove in His Hand.
Ca. 1650

Oil on canvas. 80 × 66.5 cm
Signed in monogram, right: *FH*
Received in 1754 from the J. Gotzkowsky collection, Berlin. Inv. No. 982

In his portraits Frans Hals, while trying to carefully preserve the sitter's individuality, aimed at bringing out the traits most common to the Dutch in the first post-revolutionary decades—their optimistic outlook and *joie de vivre*.

Hals' inimitable painterly manner—so full of vigour, so sweeping and unconstrained—matches the dynamic personality of the man depicted. The psychological integrity of the likeness is made all the more striking through the use of the colour scheme of exceptional tonal unity. The identity of the person portrayed has not been established, although some indirect intimations enable us to assume that he is a physician.

JACOB VAN RUISDAEL. 1628/29–1682

Dutch school

157. The Bog. *Ca.* 1665

Oil on canvas. 72.5 × 99 cm
Signed, botom left: *JV Ruisdael*
Received between 1763 and 1764. Inv. No. 934

This landscape is remarkable for its romantic uplift. It is a work in which the painter's gift of artistic generalization seem to vie with his equally formidable depth of the philosophic insight into the world of nature. The interplay of light and shade, the contrast of the pristine blue of the sky and the russet of the autumn foliage, the juxtaposing of the young, fragile shoots and the rotting, storm-crippled trees, the mirror-like smoothness of still waters and turbulent swinging of the branches—all that helps to bring out the very essence of nature, its never-ending transformations, its dying and renewal.

PETER PAUL RUBENS. 1577–1640

Flemish school

158. Portrait of a Lady in Waiting. *Ca.* 1625

Oil on canvas. 63.5 × 47.5 cm
Received in 1772 from the P. Crozat collection, Paris. Inv. No. 478

This portrait is a unique work in Rubens' *œuvre*. Owing to a remarkably lyrical character and an unusually intimate rendering of the image, the picture stands out against even the few informal portraits of the people close to the artist.

Taking in evidence the preparatory drawing (now in the Albertina, Vienna), the Hermitage painting is believed to be a representation of a lady in waiting to the Infanta Isabella, the ruler of the Netherlands. It is quite evident, however, that while working on the subject, Rubens had created an entirely new image, and he did so by gradually altering the features of his sitter to suit those of his early-deceased daughter. Painted two years before the *Lady in Waiting*, the portrait of Clara Serena Rubens (now in the collection of Charles U. Bay, New York) reveals a striking likeness to it and, thus, anticipates, as it were, the general conception of the latter.

158

PETER PAUL RUBENS. 1577–1640
Flemish school
159. The Coronation of Marie de' Medici

Oil on panel. 49 × 63 cm
Received before 1774. Inv. No. 516

This oil sketch depicts the coronation of Marie de' Medici which took place in the Paris church of St. Denis on May 13, 1610. The very fact of coronation was imparted a special importance as it secured Marie de' Medici's right to the French throne. The officiating Cardinal de Joyeuse is depicted in the act of placing the crown on the head of Marie de' Medici who is shown accompanied by the dauphin, the future king Louis XIII of France. Also attending are cardinals de Gondi and de Sourdis and four bishops. Following in the wake are a young cavalier and, somewhat further to the right, the crown princess Henrietta Maria, the future queen of England. The right half of the picture is occupied by a group of nobles with the natural sons of king Henry IV in front and queen Margaret of Valois in the rear.

In some scholars' opinion, the dog in the foreground, far from being a mere decorative device, serves as a kind of symbol recurrent in the visual arts of the sixteenth century. The dog, in fact, was regarded as endowed with an occult faculty of divining the truth and telling fortune. In this particular case its appearance could well portend an imminent assassination of king Henry IV, which was to take place the day following the coronation.

PETER PAUL RUBENS. 1577–1640
Flemish school

160. Lion Hunt. *Ca.* 1621

Oil on panel. 43 × 64 cm
Received in 1772 from the P. Crozat collection, Paris. Inv. No. 515

Rubens' oil sketches are in some ways more revealing than his "finished" productions as they provide a glimpse into the workings of creative thought of this great Flemish master.

One cannot but marvel at that tremendous force of observation with which the artist captures on canvas both the general pattern of moving masses and a minute though no less significant detail. People and beasts are caught here in one furious tangle of a life-and-death struggle and, from the look of it, one can hardly believe that in this painting, as on many other occasions, Rubens drew inspiration from the classic idiom of Leonardo's *Battle of Anghiari.*

This *Lion Hunt* is a sketch for the picture of the same title, now in the Alte Pinakothek, Munich.

JACOB JORDAENS. 1593–1678
Flemish school

161. The Bean King. *Ca.* 1638

Oil on canvas. 157 × 211 cm
Received in 1922 from the Academy of Arts Museum, Petrograd. Inv. No. 3760

The subject of the Bean King, a traditional folk festival, was varied and elaborated by Jordaens in many of his pictures. It was through these works that the artist achieved his worldwide fame. The engaging, if somewhat crude, scene is presented in this picture in all its natural flavour, with nothing to be prettied or glossed over. Its vivid colouring, built upon an endless variety of subtle flesh tints, and the dynamism of its powerful masses lend this otherwise commonplace scene the character of a truly imposing event. Jordaens, who like many true Flemings of his time, fell under Rubens' spell, which is evident in his penchant for the monumental and lofty, creates here, nevertheless, an entirely new and original type of genre painting differing from both the Caravagesque "merry companies" and the *vanitas* scenes depicted by Dutch painters.

At present, there exist several versions of *The Bean King* known to have been painted by Jordaens (Musées Royaux des Beaux-Arts de Belgique, Brussels; Gemäldegalerie, Alte Meister und Antikenabteilung, Kassel; Musée des Beaux-Arts, Valenciennes; the Louvre, Paris).

ANTHONY VAN DYCK. 1599–1641
Flemish school

162. Philadelphia and Elizabeth Wharton.
Second half of the 1630s

Oil on canvas. 162 × 130 cm
Received in 1779 from the Robert Walpole collection in Houghton Hall, England. Inv. No. 533

As regards the doubts that were at one time cast upon the true identity of the persons depicted, one can hardly distrust the inscription containing the girls'

names which was made on the canvas at the time when Lord Philip Wharton, the man who commissioned the portrait, was still alive.

The children types were always the artist's *forte*. This picture is another case in point, as here, too, for all their smart clothes and attempts at looking serious, the girls retain that lovely air of child-like innocence and naivety. The picture's colour scheme, built on a combination of light silver and blue tones, is typical of Van Dyck's later style remarkable for its elegance.

164

EL GRECO (DOMENICOS THEOTOKOPOULOS). 1541–1614
Spanish school

163, 164. St. Peter and St. Paul. 1587–92

Oil on canvas. 121.5 × 105 cm
Received in 1911 from the P. Durnovo collection, St. Petersburg. Inv. No. 390

El Greco, in much the same way as Bassano and Tintoretto before him, was noted for his predilection for elaborate foreshortenings and a palette of colours that seemed to have a luminescence of their own. Coupled with his illumination, done in hectic flashes of light, these devices imparted his pictures that peculiar turbulence that later came to be regarded as the main feature of El Greco's art. The visual imagery of this picture is built upon the contrast of two opposing themes—that of St. Paul, with his fervour and intransigence, and the meek and humble St. Peter.

DIEGO VELÁZQUEZ. 1599–1660
Spanish school

165. Count-Duke of Olivares. *Ca.* 1638

Oil on canvas. 67 × 54.5 cm
Received in 1814 from the W. Coesvelt collection, Amsterdam. Inv. No. 300

In 1623, Velázquez moved from Sevilla to Madrid where he was appointed Court Painter to King Philip IV of Spain. From that time on, the artist chiefly portrayed members of the royal family and their entourage.
Don Gaspar de Guzmán, Count of Olivares and Duke of San Lúcar (1587–1645), was from 1621 to 1643 a minister in the Spanish government. This all-powerful favourite of Philip IV had often his official portraits painted by Velázquez. The Hermitage painting, however, marks·the beginning of a new phase in the artist's creative evolution. The minister's cunning, vulturine face has here a tense expression, his eyes have a skeptical rather than confident look; deathly pale and bloated, this face, with its cheeks flabby and eyelids swollen, and its massive bill of a nose, gives Olivares a look of the man far gone in years, and also the one whose fortune is ebbing. The portrait, nonetheless, retains all the significance of the person portrayed.
The picture's colouring is very restrained. Deep, yet expressive, is the black of the costume set off against an olive-green, partially illuminated background. The white collar stands out, delicate and light, against a generally sombre tonality. The face, rendered in flowing brushstrokes, is brilliantly modelled.

FRANCISCO DE ZURBARÁN. 1598–1644
Spanish school

166. The Girlhood of the Virgin Mary. *Ca.* 1660

Oil on canvas. 73.5 × 53.5 cm
Received in 1814 from the W. Coesvelt collection, Amsterdam. Inv. No. 306

Zurbarán often turned for inspiration to the theme of Mary's childhood which he discovered in the late 1620s, and continued to elaborate it for the rest of his life. The Hermitage version is said to have been inspired by the text of the Pseudo-Gospel of Matthew.
Mary, portrayed here as a tender child, has laid down her needlework and is saying grace, her features lit up with profoundest emotion. Despite a somewhat narrow concept of the subject and a restrained use of expressive means (the figure of the girl stands out against a dark, neutral background with a minimum of accessories), this small-size picture is remarkable for its feeling for monumentality made more pronounced through its static composition, the figure's monolithic silhouette, and the details of the dress rendered in bold heavy masses.
The picture's colouring, with its prevalence of bright, contrasting colours, resembles that of mediaeval paintings and, especially, painted wood sculpture. Zurbarán retained this predilection for a saturated local colour, which he derived from his early experience of painting statues, throughout his life. The work reveals his great attention to detail. The eye is immediately drawn to the delicate embroidery on the collar and cuffs of Mary's dress.

165

BARTOLOMÉ ESTEBAN MURILLO. 1617–1682
Spanish school

167. Boy with a Dog. 1650s

Oil on canvas. 74 × 60 cm
Received in 1772 from the Duke de Choiseul collection, Paris. Inv. No. 386

This is one of Murillo's finest genre paintings of the 1650s. A companion piece, *Girl Fruit-seller*, is in the Pushkin Museum of Fine Arts, Moscow. Murillo's *Boy with a Dog* caught the fancy of Edouard Manet, who painted a picture on the same subject (Rothschield-Goldschmidt collection, Paris).

FRANCISCO JOSÉ DE GOYA Y LUCIENTES. 1746–1828
Spanish school
168. Portrait of the Actress Antonia Zárate. *Ca.* 1811

Oil on canvas. 71 × 58 cm
Received in 1972 as a gift of Armand Hammer (USA). Inv. No. 10198

Intransigence in his aesthetic appraisal of the world and a passionate devotion to his ideals—these are the two main facets of Goya's art. His handling of the subject, especially in portraits, never leaves one in doubt as to where the painter's sympathies lie: the attitude of a nonchalant observer is utterly foreign to his artistic idiom.
Antonia Zárate (1775–1811), actress of the Madrid theatre, shared the artist's spiritual aspirations. Goya had already painted her once, in 1805 (private collection, Blessington, Ireland). In this portrait the artist skilfully conveyed an air of frailty enveloping the young woman's features, the pallor of her face, and that haunted look of her big wistful eyes betraying, as it were, the imminence of her tragic end: sick with consumption, the actress died soon after the completion of the portrait.

LUCAS CRANACH THE ELDER. 1472–1553
German school
169, 170. Venus and Cupid

Oil on canvas (transferred from panel). 213 × 102 cm
Left-hand side, in the middle: monogram *LC,* the sign of a winged snake,
and the date, *1509*
Received between 1763 and 1774. Inv. No. 680

A great master of the German Renaissance, Lucas Cranach the Elder embodied in this Venus type his own ideal of female beauty and his conception of a perfect human figure. His picture was, in fact, the first attempt in northern European art at depicting the antique goddess nude. Cranach's Venus is a tall, long-legged woman with a small head and a beautiful, if somewhat angular, body. The sweeping rhythm and elegance of the silhouette—features that were inherited by the artist from Late Gothic art—imbue the figure with an unusual charm.
The painting testifies to a considerable latitude of Cranach's interests, his close spiritual affinity to the Humanist ideas that were gaining ground in sixteenth-century Germany. This theme, one of the most widespread in the art of the Italian Renaissance, is given here an intrinsically German interpretation. Italian artists, for whom the image of Venus was the quintessence of femininity, saw nothing reprehensible in portraying the naked body which they openly glorified as the ideal of sensuous beauty and grace. Unlike the Italians, Cranach tries to impart his depiction a moralistic tinge, warning the viewer against earthly temptations, which he does in the form of the following Latin verse inscribed in the upper part of his picture:
Pelle Cupidineos Toto Conamine Luxus
Ne Tue Possideat Pectora Ceca Venus
(Study with all your might to resist the voluptuous Cupid
Lest blind Love master your captive heart).
The colour scheme of the picture is a subtle combination of yellow and golden tones for the figures with only the red beads around Cupid's neck standing out sharply against the dark background.
There are a great number of extant versions of the picture executed either by the artist himself, or by his numerous pupils, followers, and imitators. In 1509 Lucas Cranach the Elder produced the woodcut on the same theme which slightly differed from the original in details, and had a landscape as its background.

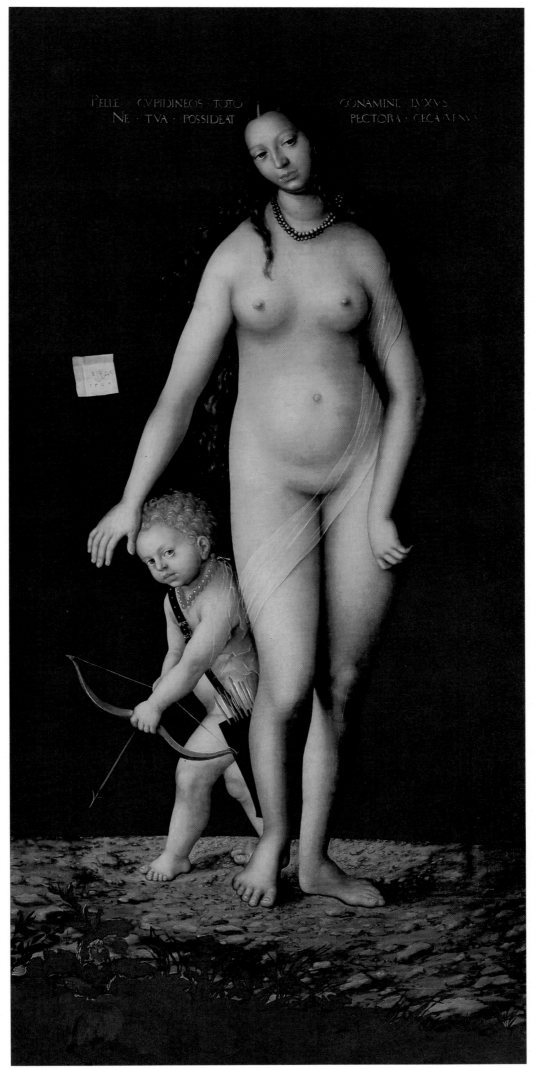

171

ALBRECHT DÜRER. 1471–1528
German school

171. The Virgin and Child

Charcoal on paper. 42 × 24 cm (cut off on all sides, especially
at the bottom)
Received in 1924 from the I. Betskoi collection, Academy of Arts,
Petrograd. Inv. No. 15378

Done before 1515, the drawing is a detail of a cartoon
for the stained-glass window in the chapel of the Pfinzing family in St. Sebald Church in Nuremberg. The
stained-glass panel was executed in the second half of
1515 in the workshop of Veit Hirschvogel in memory

of Siegfried Pfinzing who died in 1514. Dürer used the
drawing, with slight alterations, again for the woodcut
The Certosa Virgin, dated 1515 (J. Meder, *Dürer-Kata-
log*, Vienna, 1932, No. 210).
Keeping in mind the importance of the commission,
the artist took special care when drawing the cartoon
(for example, he used a pair of compasses to draw the
haloes).

172

AMBROSIUS HOLBEIN. *Ca.* 1495—*ca.* 1519
German school

172. Portrait of a Young Man

Tempera on panel. 44 × 32.5 cm
Monogram of interwined letters *AHB* (Ambrosius Holbein Basileusis?) on a shield in the garland, top right; inscribed and dated in cartouche, mid-left, near the column: *Etatis. sve. XX MDXVIII* (at the age of twenty, 1518)
Received *ca.* 1773. Inv. No. 685

Originally, the portrait was probably the right wing of a diptych. It was painted soon after the artist's arrival in Basel. In the nineteenth century, Heinrich Waagen ascribed it to Hans Holbein the Younger. A version (or an old copy?) of the portrait, formerly in the Van der Berg collection, is now in the collection of J. C. de Baeck (Schoten, Belgium).

235

173

ÉTIENNE BOBILLET and PAUL DE MOSSELMAN.
Active mid-fifteenth century
The Netherlands

173. The Mourner. *Ca.* 1450–56

Marble. Height 42.2 cm
Received in 1884 from the A. Basilewsky collection,
Paris. Inv. No. H. ск. 322

This mid-fifteenth century statuette was made for the tomb of the Duke Jean de Berry in St. Chapelle at Bourges. Works by Bobillet and Mosselman are marked by poignant emotionality reaching at times the intensity of ecstatic exaltation—a feature, though, fairly typical of mid-fifteenth century Netherlandish art in general.

The figure of the mourner is imbued with an unusual expressiveness. His cloak comes down in deep unfurling folds, hands are crossed on his chest in a gesture of renunciation. His face is fully hidden behind the hood, but his bowed head betrays a sustained anguish.

MONOGRAMMIST IP.
Active in the 1520s
Austria

174. The Lamentation. *Ca.* 1520–25

Wood. 19.5 × 15.5 cm
Signed below: *IP*
Received in 1919 from the Society for the Encouragement of Arts, Petrograd. Inv. No. 1540

The monogrammist IP was active in the 1520s in the Salzburg area. The signed works by this master are extremely rare. His artistic idiom, like that of his contemporary artists, is marked by an extensive use of landscape motifs. The Hermitage relief is no exception—the group of mourners is portrayed against a landscape background. The rendering of this relief shows a virtuoso hand: despite its small dimensions, the work retains its monumental quality.

CASPAR DAVID FRIEDRICH. 1774–1840
German school
175. On a Sailing Ship. 1818–20

Oil on canvas. 71 × 56 cm
Received in 1958 from the Peterhof Palace, near Leningrad. Inv. No. 9773

This picture was painted by Friedrich after he had travelled with his wife to Greifswald, his birthplace in North Germany. The painting, therefore, is in a way a depiction of an episode from the artist's life. Yet, at the same time, it is a highly symbolic work: sailing at sea signifies treading the path of life, while the town looming on the horizon through the misty air suggests a resting-place the man is bound for after his life-long wanderings in the world. Friedrich's architectural motif has no counterpart in reality, being a blend of different buildings from Stralsund, Greifswald, and Dresden. Extant are some preparatory drawings for the picture (National Gallery, Oslo).

238

THOMAS GAINSBOROUGH. 1727–1788

English school

176. Portrait of a Lady in Blue. Late 1770s

Oil on canvas. 76 × 64 cm
Received between 1912 and 1916 from the A. Khitrovo collection, Petrograd, as the owner's bequest. Inv. No. 3509

The *Portrait of a Lady in Blue* belongs to the most accomplished works by Gainsborough. A peculiar life-like quality of this captivating image is due to the precision and sense of rhythm with which the graceful half-length figure, with its pale blue, pink, white, light brown, and pearl-grey tones, is inscribed in the rectangle of the canvas. This, and the beauty of Gainsborough's brushwork, light and vibrant, capable of conveying an almost indiscernible movement, impart the picture its unusual poetic charm.
The superlative mastery of this portrait's execution indicates that it must have been painted by the artist at the height of his powers. His preference for radiant blue tonality places the picture in the 1770s or '80s, which is furthermore confirmed by the lady's costume and her coiffure of fluffed-up, powdered hair topped with a tiny trimmed hat and ostrich feathers.
For a long time the painting was thought to be a portrait of the Duchess of Beaufort, but there has been no proof to support this identification.

English school

177. A Knight of the Order of the Garter

Black and white chalk on grey paper. 66 × 33.5 cm
Received in 1768 from the K. Cobenzl collection, Brussels. Inv. No. 5926

Although the tradition of ascribing this drawing to Peter Lely goes back to the first half of the eighteenth century, it was catalogued in the Cobenzl collection and, later, in that of the Hermitage as the work of Anthony van Dyck. The former attribution was re-established by Mikhail Dobroklonsky. The drawing is one of a set of character studies from the *Grand Procession of the Sovereign and the Knight Companies on the Day of St. George*, dated about 1663–71. Sixteen sheets of this set, bound together in an album, were sold at an auction in Amsterdam on March 23, 1763, whereupon they found their way into various collections of the world (the Rijksprentenkabinet in Amsterdam; the Kupferstichkabinett in Berlin; the Albertina in Vienna; the Ashmolean Museum in Oxford; the Crooker Art Gallery in Sacramento, Ca.; collections of Robert Witt, Van Ehgen, Frits Lugt, Lord Northbrook, and others). The figure in the Hermitage drawing is the same as on the sheet in Amsterdam, where it is shown from the back. About thirty such drawings are currently known.

178

JOHN RUSSELL. 1745–1806
English school

178. Portrait of Mrs. Janet Grizel Cuming

Signed and dated, upper right: *J. Russel R. A. p^t 1794*
Pastel on paper mounted on canvas. 59 × 44 cm
Received in 1935 from the Boyarsky collection; earlier, the A. Khitrovo collection. Inv. No. 42323

As indicated in the form of an inscription on the reverse of the portrait, the subject is Janet Grizel, the thirty-six year old eldest daughter of George Chalmers of Pittencrieff, and the wife of the Edinburgh banker Thomas Cuming Earnside.

A highly versatile painter and engraver, as well as author of a fundamental treatise on the work in pastel,

John Russell was able, with his virtuoso touch, to overcome the natural density of pastel brushstroke. Working the outline with hatches of black and white chalk and shading the pastel powder over the flat surface of paper, the artist arrives at a great tonal subtlety and such a translucence of colour that the painting seems to be a gossamer of light and air. Owing to his well thought-out technique, Russell's works are, in most cases, in good state of preservation and thus refute the widespread notion of pastel as a fragile, short-lived medium.

JEAN GOUJON (?) 1510–1568
France

179. Venus and Cupid. 1550s

Marble. 51 × 57 cm
Received in 1926 from the former Museum of the Stieglitz School of Art
and Industrial Design, Leningrad. Inv. No. H. ск. 907

The relief is traditionally ascribed to Jean Goujon, one
of the foremost French sculptors of the sixteenth century whose output also includes such notable works as
the sculptural decor of the Louvre courtyard façade
and the Nymphs of the Fountain of the Innocents in
Paris.
The Hermitage relief is believed to have come from the
Château Anet for which Goujon, while working on
commission from king Henri II of France, executed a
number of decorative panels. The figures are so skilfully spaced within the oval that the outlines of their
supple bodies and the draperies seem to echo its curving shape. An expressive treatment of elongated figures, smooth and flowing linear design, and a virtuoso
handling of the marble texture, all makes this relief
one of the finest works by Goujon.

ÉTIENNE MAURICE FALCONET.
1716–1791
France

180. Flora. *Ca.* 1770

Marble. Height 32 cm
Received in 1926 from the Yusupov collection, Leningrad. Inv. No. 1261

Before coming to Russia, where he produced the monument to Peter the Great in St. Petersburg, Falconet
had been mostly known for his elegant statuettes in
marble and porcelain. The sculptor's rare gift was his
marvellous ability to combine the clarity of design
with the refinement of form and gesture. Grace never
turns finicky in his works and their lyricism is never
allowed to grow into cheap sentimentality. This little
statuette of seated Flora—the goddess of flowers—is
very typical of the master's idiom. The figure is well
arranged in space, showing to advantage the graceful
linear pattern of the silhouette and a gently, yet confi-
dently modelled form.

ANTOINE WATTEAU.
1684–1721

French school

181. An Embarrassing Proposal.
Ca. 1716

Oil on canvas. 65 × 84.5 cm
Received in 1769 from the Count H. Brühl
collection, Dresden. Inv. No. 1150

This canvas belongs to a series of
paintings created by Watteau in a
style known as *fêtes galantes*. The
picture epitomizes, as it were, the
artist's dream of an idyllic, arcadian
world; there is also here, as in many
of Watteau's works, an air of genuine melancholy which seems to deny
the very possibility of such an ideal.

246

182

JEAN HONORÉ FRAGONARD. 1732–1806
French school

182. The Stolen Kiss. 1780s

Oil on canvas. 45 × 55 cm
Received in 1895 from the Lazienki Palace, Warsaw, in exchange for
La Polonaise by Antoine Watteau. Inv. No. 1300

The Stolen Kiss is surely one of the most captivating works by Fragonard.
Made in a style of *scènes galantes*, the painting reveals the influence of the
French Enlightenment painters Greuze and Chardin as well as the artist's
debt to the seventeenth-century Dutch Masters. Whatever he aims to
convey on canvas—be it the brilliance of a young woman's silk dress or the
transparency of her light scarf, the lustre of the table surface or the velvety
sheen of the carpet—all shows a meticulous attention to detail and an
almost Dutch-like approach to colour and form.

It was a fashion with the French painters of the 1770s and '80s to produce
thematically linked pictures in series. A case in point is Greuze who thus
managed to compile a regular novel out of a series of canvases. Fragonard,
too, painted a pendant to the Hermitage piece entitled *The Contract*,
thereby bringing to a happy ending the adventures of his heroes.

EUGÈNE DELACROIX. 1798–1863
French school

185. Lion Hunt in Morocco. 1854

Oil on canvas. 74 × 92 cm
Received in 1922 from the Academy of Arts, Petrograd.
Inv. No. 3853

The journey to Morocco and Algeria, made by Delacroix in 1832, was to remain for him a source of inspiration throughout many years of his career as an artist. Thus, in 1855, he painted a large canvas *The Lion Hunt* (now in the Musée de Beaux-Arts, Bordeaux). This major work was preceded by a number of smaller-size paintings and studies of which the Hermitage piece is undoubtedly the finest. However, unlike the Bordeaux canvas where it is the actual kill that is given the prominence, that of the Hermitage highlights the moment, no less tense and dramatic, preceding the encounter. It is an extremely dynamic composition, which is achieved by employing a variety of painterly means: the colour scheme built on juxtaposing the saturated red with blue and green, the brushwork, which is free and untrammelled, and the line distorting the form to capture the imminence of rapid movement. One cannot but believe the artist writing of a "fit of an inspired rage" he was caught in when working on that picture.

252

CLAUDE MONET. 1840–1926
French school

186. Lady in the Garden. 1867

Oil on canvas. 80 × 99 cm
Received in 1930 from the Museum of Modern Western Art, Moscow.
Formerly in the S. Shchukin collection, Moscow. Inv. No. 6505

The picture was painted at Sainte-Adresse and thus dates from Monet's Pre-Impressionist period. Compositionally, it falls into three clearly discernible parts: the tree in blossom and a flower-bed in the centre, thick foliage in the backround, and a strip of sun-lit lawn in the forefront. However, the artist's treatment of leaves and flowers, rendered in generalized manner and by strokes of the brush butt may be regarded as the first manifestation of his Impressionist technique.

A radiograph of the picture has revealed a male figure, which was originally depicted at the lady's right and subsequently overpainted by the artist.

187

ÉDOUARD MANET. 1832–1883
French school

187. Portrait of Madame Julies Guillemet

Signed, bottom right corner: *E. M.*
Black chalk on paper. 313 × 220 cm
Received in 1938 from a private collection. Inv. No. 43094

This drawing is a study for the pastel portrait of Madame Guillemet (St. Louis Art Museum, St. Louis), who repeatedly sat for Manet, appearing, for example, in his painting *In the Hothouse* (Staatliche Museen, Berlin; dated 1880), as well as in his pencil drawings, pastels, and watercolours. What the artist strove to achieve was not only an individual likeness, but rather a generalized image of the young "Parisienne", as Manet called one of his portraits (Ordrupgaardsamlingen, Charlottenlund). With a few swift, bold strokes the artist created a charming image of a young woman, who seems to have flashed for an instant before his eyes, leaving a vague yet indelible imprint.

PIERRE-AUGUSTE RENOIR. 1841–1919

French school

188. Woman in Black. *Ca.* 1876

Oil on canvas. 63 × 53 cm
Signed, middle right: *A. Renoir*
Received in 1930 from the Museum of Modern Western Art, Moscow.
Formely, the S. Shchukin collection, Moscow. Inv. No. 6506

Renoir, who was unrivalled in his ability to capture the charm and fascination of Parisiennes, makes he   an extremely fine character study of his model. His main concern is with colour, pre-eminently the black one, whose rich pictorial potentialities he seeks to bring out. The colour range of the sitter's dress is devoid of monotony: only in the shadows is the pure black discernible, whilst all the rest is a subtle interplay of fine gradations of grey, from ashen, bordering on black, to the silvery *gorge-de-pigeon*.

It still has not been established who is portrayed in this painting; the attempt made to identify the woman in black with "la belle Anna", a Monmartre model of some repute, was not corroborated by the later research.

189

PIERRE-AUGUSTE RENOIR. 1841–1919

French school

189. Portrait of the Actress Jeanne Samary. 1878

Oil on canvas. 173 × 103 cm
Received in 1948 from the Museum of Modern Western Art, Moscow. Formerly, the M. Morozov collection, Moscow. Inv. No. 9003

Jeanne Samary (1857–1890) was a well-known actress of the Comédie Française. This representative portrait depicting the actress in an evening dress in the foyer of the theatre was Renoir's official entry for the 1879 Salon, which would explain a somewhat conventionalized treatment of the model. This circumstance, however, is in no way depriving the portrait of its spontaneity and vividness. The yellowish-pink of the dress is fully in harmony with the warmth and freshness of the model's pearly-pink skin, and adds to the sparkle in her blue eyes.

PAUL CÉZANNE. 1839–1906

French school

190. Still Life with Curtain. *Ca.* 1899

Oil on canvas. 53 × 72 cm
Received in 1930 from the Museum of Modern Western Art, Moscow. Formerly, in the S. Shchukin collection, Moscow. Inv. No. 6514

The painting, based upon the principles of inner rhythm and unity, is typical of Cézanne's later style when the artist began to overcome the static character of his earlier works. Here, the artist juxtaposes the fruits as material objects endowed with definite shape, mass, and volume and the linen table-cloth with its subtle interplay of haphazard forms. In still lifes such as this one Cézanne's painstaking study of nature and his yearning to uncover its fundamental laws find its ultimate expression. Like most of works by Cézanne, the *Still Life with Curtain* can be dated only approximately. It is known that in autumn 1899, while staying in Paris, the artist did a series of large-size still lifes. The Hermitage canvas is evidently one of them.

191

VINCENT VAN GOGH. 1853–1890
Dutch school
191. The Lilac Bush. 1889

Oil on canvas. 73 × 92 cm
Received in 1930 from the Museum of Modern Western Art, Moscow.
Formerly, the S. Shchukin collection, Moscow. Inv. No. 6511

The painting was executed in the hospital of Saint-Rémy. It was one of the pictures Van Gogh mentioned working on in a letter to his brother Théo dated May 9, 1889: "I have been doing two new subjects which I discovered right here in the garden—purple irises and a lilac bush." The impact of Van Gogh's vivid colouring and an intense dynamic quality of texture is such that the viewer seems to be actually re-living the rustle of leaves and puffs of air on a hot day in southern France.

192, 193 ▶

VINCENT VAN GOGH. 1853–1890
Dutch school
192, 193. Ladies of Arles. 1888

Oil on canvas. 73 × 92 cm
Received in 1948 from the Museum of Modern Western Art, Moscow.
Formerly, the S. Shchukin collection, Moscow. Inv. No. 9116

The picture was painted in Arles at a time when Van Gogh shared his lodgings with Gauguin. The influence of the latter, and also of the Pont-Aven school in general, is felt both in the overall design and in Van Gogh's particular emphasis on the outline, and his generalized treatment of form. However, the artist's brushwork is entirely individual: the pigments are laid in impasto, with multi-directional strokes. In his search for an enhanced colour vibrancy Van Gogh resorts to juxtaposition of contrasting tones.

PAUL GAUGUIN. 1848–1903
French school

194. Pastorales Tahitiennes. 1892–93

Oil on canvas. 86 × 113 cm
Received in 1948 from the Museum of Modern Western Art, Moscow.
Formerly, the I. Morozov collection, Moscow. Inv. No. 9119

Gauguin resolved this painting as a kind of decorative panel where the fluid rhythms of linear arabesques are in keeping with harmoniously juxtaposed colour planes. The artist dated it 1893, although the picture was painted the previous year.

PABLO PICASSO. 1881–1973
French school

195. Boy with a Dog. 1905

Gouache on cardboard. 57 × 41 cm
Received in 1934 from the Museum of Modern Western Art, Moscow.
Formerly, the S. Shchukin collection, Moscow. Inv. No. 42158

This drawing is one of the studies for a composition with a group of wandering circus artists, which was started in Paris at the end of 1904, but is itself a work of high artistic merit. To the same series belongs a version, very close to the Hermitage study, with two acrobats, one of which is the Hermitage boy, and with the same dog (Museum of Modern Art, New York). The New York study was done not later than February 1905, since from February 25 to March 6 it was exhibited at the Cerurrier Gallery and on May 15 it was reproduced in Apollinaire's article in *La Plume*. The Hermitage gouache must have beem done at an earlier stage, presumably immediately before the New York study.

In the process of work on the study the artist's concept changed several times, which led to changes in the conceived composition. The final version, *Family of Saltimbanques* (National Gallery of Art, Washington), does not contain the figures mentioned above. The existence of an earlier variant with the two acrobats and the dog can be proved only by an x-ray photograph of the Washington painting, where these figures are perceivable through the upper layer of paint. It can be surmised that in the course of his work on the composition Picasso decided to give up the subject related to the world of paupers, to which the boy depicted in both studies apparently belonged.

196

PABLO PICASSO. 1881–1973
French school
196. Woman with a Fan (After the Ball). 1908

Oil on canvas. 150 × 101 cm
Received in 1934 from the Museum of Modern Western Art, Moscow.
Formerly, the S. Shchukin collection, Moscow. Inv. No. 7705

The motif of a woman resting after a ball is a fairly frequent one in art catering for the tastes of aristocratic salons. This hackneyed idiom is turned into ridicule by Picasso who contrasts it with his own image full of barbaric force and primordial simplicity. The woman's figure is reminiscent of a piece of primitive wooden sculpture. Some parts of her body are reduced to elemental geometric forms, to mutually contrasting arcs and angles. The asymmetry of her shoulders heralds the approach of "simultaneity", i.e. the contemporaneous presentation of different views of an object—a device the artist was to develop at a later stage of his career.

HENRI MATISSE. 1869–1954
French school
197. The Dance. 1910

Oil on canvas. 260 × 391 cm
Received in 1948 from the Museum of Modern Western Art, Moscow.
Formerly, the S. Shchukin collection, Moscow. Inv. No. 9673

The two decorative panels *The Dance* and *Music* rank among Matisse's best creations. *The Dance* was the first to be designed and realized by the artist. Its chief motif—a ring of dancing nudes—appears in Matisse's earlier, 1906 painting *The Joy of Living* where it constitutes its central part.
The hightened expressiveness of *The Dance* is achieved through an extreme intensification and synthesis of painterly means. The three primary colours employed—blue, pink, and green—are brought here to the highest pitch of vibrancy. The figures are shown caught in a whirlwind of tempestuous dancing, but for all its fury the picture never loses a sense of measure and harmony as its two opposing forces—centrifugal and centripetal—are perfectly balanced within its space.
The preparatory material consists of three charcoal drawings (Musée de Peinture et de Sculpture, Grenoble, and two private collections, Paris), and a sketch in oils (Museum of Modern Art, New York).

198

199

198. Reliquary of St. Elizabeth of Hungary

France. Mid-13th century
Wood, copper, silver, gemstones, glass; chased, embossed, filigreed, and nielloed. Height 58 cm
Received in 1885 from the A. Basilewsky collection, Paris. Inv. No. Φ 108

The reliquary of St. Elizabeth of Hungary is a work of art belonging to an age which was marked by transition from the Romanesque to the Gothic. It contains the relics of the Hungarian princess Elizabeth, wife of Ludwig, the landgrave of Thuringia. She died in 1231, and was canonized in 1235. In its design, the reliquary resembles numerous vessels of the same kind which were produced in German Lorraine. However, the inscriptions, made in French, suggest that it was executed in France, probably in Picardy.

199. Clasp with the Virgin and Saints. 15th century

Germany. By Derick
Parcel-gilt copper and silver; cast, chased, and engraved. Height 21.5 cm
Received in 1885 from the A. Basilewsky collection, Paris. Inv. No. Φ 153

The inscription on the reverse of the clasp discloses to us the name of its maker, master Derick, who was probably active somewhere in Lower Saxony. The clasp is remarkable for its elaborate multi-petalled shape which perfectly blends the central part with its pointed arcade and the petals bearing misic-making angels. The somewhat cumbersome figures of saints stand in marked contrast to those of angels, light and vivacious, and also to the delicately finished musical instruments.

200

200, 201. Set of plates: *scudello* and *tondino*. *Ca.* 1550

Urbino, Italy. Workshop of Fontana
Majolica, with painted decoration. Diameter 20.5 cm (*scudello*) and 19 cm (*tondino*)
Received—*scudello*: 1920 from the M. Botkin collection, Petrograd; *tondino*:
1885 from the A. Basilewsky collection, Paris, Inv. Nos. Ф 1692 and Ф 395

This set consisting of two small plates was used in the ceremony of congratulating a mother on child birth. The larger plate, *scudello*, was intended for soup, while the smaller one, *tondino*, which could also serve as a lid, was used for bread and sweets. The *tondino* shows a scene, *The Childbirth*. The scene takes its central part, while the remaining space is painted with an exquisite grotesque ornament typical of the period.

201

202

202. Pendant: *Caravel*

Spain. First half of the 16th century
Emerald, set in gold and painted in enamels.
Length 10 cm
Provenance unknown. Inv. No. 314

Pendants are rare among the objects of Spanish jewellery, although as far back as the sixteenth century Spain was renowned for its rich and diverse jewellery ornaments which were often studded with gemstones brought from the West Indies.

The caravel motif came to be associated with the era of Great Geographic Discoveries, and that of pirates and filibusters. The Hermitage sample is made of a magnificent piece of emerald of about 125 carats. An exclusive transparence, beauty, depth, and the tonal brightness of the stone suggest its Columbian origin.

203. Covered vase. 17th century

Maria, Andalusia (Spain)
Bluish-green glass. Height 32 cm
Received in 1923 from the former Museum of the Stieglitz School of Art and Industrial Design, Petrograd. First Branch of the Hermitage Museum. Inv. No. K 1977

This four-handled vase is a fine specimen of Andalusian art glass in which folk traditions and Oriental influence were closely interwoven. The decoration is typical of folk art—it combines threading, chain and pincered trailing, cresting, and rings suspended from loops. Its shape, however, is associated with fourteenth-century Syrian mosque lamps and Hispano-Moresque pottery of the first half of the sixteenth century. The multi-handled vases were widespread in the southern provinces of Spain in the sixteenth to the eighteenth century.

274

204. Cameo: *Portrait of Antoine Perrenot de Granvelle*

Italy. Second half of the 16th century
Chalcedonyx, mounted in gold and decorated with diamond. 4.8 × 2.6 cm
Received in 1795 from the Thomas Martin collection, London.
Inv. No. 1020

The image on the gem is a repetition of the portrait of the Cardinal de Granvelle on the obverse of a 1558 medal—the work of a famous Italian engraver, medallist, and sculptor Leone Leoni, who was for some time active at the Spanish court. All this gives sufficient ground for attributing the cameo to Leoni's own hand, or, at least, to the carvers of his circle. This medal served as a model for making several replicas of the portrait in stone of which the one most closely resembling the Hermitage gem, although, probably of a somewhat later date, is the cameo that appeared, at

one time or other, in the British collections of the Earl of Arundel, the Duke of Marlborough, and Newton Robinson.

205. Cameo: *Lot and His Daughters*

Nuremberg, Germany. 1540–45. By Peter Flötner (?). *Ca.* 1485–1546
Chalcedonyx mounted in gold. 4.2 × 5.2 cm
Received in 1794 through the agency of Livio, St. Petersburg. Inv. No. 699

This cameo may be regarded as a genuine triumph of German Renaissance glyptics. Its virtuoso rendering of the subject-matter and the complete analogy it exhibits to an identical relief on box-wood (now in the British Museum, London) and a bronze plaquette cast from it (Würtemberg Landesmuseum, Stuttgart), both undoubtedly the works by Peter Flötner, make its present attribution highly feasible.

277

207

208

206. The Housewife. 1760–64

Frankenthal, Germany. After a model by Johann Friedrich von
Lück (1728/29–1797)
Porcelain, painted in colours. Height 16 cm
Received in 1918 from the A. Dolgorukov collection, Petrograd.
Inv. No. 13912

Statuettes occupy the leading place among the wares of the Frankenthal Porcelain Factory. A large
group of first-rate sculptors, Johann Friedrich von
Lück among them, worked here evolving models
for porcelain figurines. Von Lück held a post of
modeller at the factory from 1758 to 1764, and
turned out a large number of objects of widely
varying subject-matter.
The Housewife is one of his rarest and most attrative
pieces. The master often worked from prints: thus,
the present figurine was modelled on Jacques Philip-
pe Lebas' engraving from a painting by Jean-
Baptiste Chardin.

207, 208. Snuff-box

Paris, France, 1745–46. By Louis Urbain Thévenot
Tortoise-shell and gold. Length 8.6 cm
Received in 1789. Inv. No. 4181

The dark backround of tortoise-shell makes a contrast with the softly chased gold plaques depicting
military scenes, and a zigzag *piqué* ornamentation
running down in a rhythmic pattern.

209. Chased gold necessaire on a châtelaine with two *étui*, inlaid with heliotrope and decorated in rocaille set with diamonds and rubies

England. Mid-18th century. Length 18.9 cm
Received from a private collection. Inv. No. 1870

In the mid-eighteenth century London became one
of the leading centres of jewellery.
This necessaire, done by a first-class lapidary, is
remarkable for its high colouristic and plastic qualities. Its rocailles, bright and massive, impart the
article an unusual expressiveness. The masterly fa-
ceting of the gemstones testifies to an exceptional
skill of the goldsmith.

209

210. Dish. 17th century

Delft, Holland. The "Greek A" factory.
By Samuel van Eenhoorn. Active 1674–86
Faience, painted in cobalt blue. 45.5 × 57 cm
Received in 1923 from the former Museum of the
Stieglitz School of Art and Industrial Design,
Petrograd. Inv. No. 1187

This dish, the work of an outstanding Dutch potter Samuel van Eenhoorn, is a real masterpiece of delft-
ware. Although markedly touched
by his creative imagination, Van

210

Eenhoorn's works were largely done in imitation of Chinese porcelain. The wares are thin-walled, coated with shiny bluish-white glaze and painted in cobalt blue of soft, melting tones. In places, the outlines of the pattern blur and run into the glaze, lending it a shade of lilac, which greatly adds to the beauty of the monochrome design.

JOSIAH WEDGWOOD. 1730–1795
England
211. The "Green Frog" Service. 1773–4
Sauce-boat on stand, with spoon

Creamware, painted in colours
Received in 1910.Inv. No. 8492

The "Green Frog" service owes its name to the representation of a frog in a triangular crest, which showed that the set was intended for the Chesme Palace situated near St. Petersburg, in a locality called Kekerekeksi (the Finnish for a frog bog).

This large dinner and dessert set, consisting of 952 pieces and intended for 50 persons, was commissioned by Catherine the Great from the celebrated English ceramic artist Josiah Wedgwood. The service is made of a special variety of thin-walled faience, known as creamware, which was developed and patented by Wedgwood. The shapes were designed by the sculptor John Flaxman, and Wedgwood himself.

As follows from the inscription on one of the pieces, the service was painted with "1244 Real Views of Great Britain".

212. Tapestry: *Wisdom*

Brussels, Flanders. Early 16th century
Wool and silk. 385 × 232 cm
Received in 1923 from the former Museum of the Stieglitz School of Art and Industrial Design, Petrograd. Inv. No. T-2932

The character of its design and the treatment of the figures and the border point to Brussels as the most probable venue of the execution of this tapestry, and give ground for dating it to the early sixteenth century. The tapestry is evidently one from the series depicting Virtues. Also in the Hermitage collection is a pendant tapestry, *Justice*.

212

213. Tapestry: *Cleopatra's Feast.*
From *The History of Antony and Cleopatra* series. Second half of the 17th century

Brussels, Flanders. Workshop of Wilhelm (Guillem) van Leefdael
Wool and silk. 400 × 378 cm
Received in 1924 from the Petrograd Society for Art Treasures. Inv. No. T 2941

The cartoons for this series were executed in 1661 by Justus van Egmont (1601–1674). The series was frequently reproduced in the seventeenth century.

The design shows an episode from the story of Antony and Cleopatra: to impress Antony with her riches, Cleopatra is dissolving a priceless pearl in a goblet filled with vinegar. The monumental quality of the design with its large figures in relief, rich folds of drapery and clothes, its wide border, and a vivid colour scheme are all typical of the Flemish Baroque tapestry.

214. Centrepiece. 1718–20

Augsburg, Germany. By Johann Ludwig Biller II and Johann Jacob Bruglocher I
Received from the Winter Palace collection, St. Petersburg. Before 1742, the Biron collection, St. Petersburg. Inv. No. 8615

The first quarter of the eighteenth century saw the flourishing of silverwork in Augsburg. This centrepiece formed part of the so-called "Riga Service" and was brought to Russia in the early 1740s. It was then that the cartouches containing the Russian Empress Elizabeth's monogram were made on its tray. This fine article, produced in the workshop of the Billers, an eminent family of silversmiths, demonstrates not only technical brilliance of execution but also its makers' remarkable artistic talent.

RUSSIAN CULTURE

The Hermitage's Department of the History of Russian Culture, unlike most of its other departments which have a history of over two hundred years, has only celebrated its forty-sixth anniversary: it was organized in April—May 1941.

The department's collection began with the thousands of relics of Russian culture and art long housed in the Winter Palace and the rich collection which took shape in the early post-revolutionary years in the Department of the History of Daily Life in the Russian Museum and which consisted of numerous works of art from palaces, mansions, private collections, and small museums. New entries now come mostly from archaeological excavations which first began in 1948, as well as expeditions sent out with the express purpose of locating and acquiring relics of Russian culture and works of applied and folk art. Icons, pottery, wood-carvings, textiles, and folk costumes were brought from expeditions to the Arkhangelsk, Murmansk, Yaroslavl, Vladimir, Leningrad, and other regions. Some exhibits enter the Hermitage through its Purchasing Commission.

The department's large collection of art relics, over 300,000 pieces in all, enables us to trace the evolution of the versatile culture of the Russian people over almost 1,500 years—from the sixth to the twentieth century. The collection is subdivided into two parts: ancient Russian art (sixth to seventeenth century) and works dating from the eighteenth to the early twentieth century.

The art of Old Russia and Muscovy is illustrated mainly by archaeological finds from excavations in Kiev (tenth to twelfth century), Novgorod (tenth to fifteenth century), in the vicinity of the old Russian town of Iziaslavl (twelfth and early thirteenth centuries), and others. Interesting finds characterizing the life and customs of urban communities in Old Russia are being provided by ongoing archaeological digs in Pskov which the department has been conducting since 1954. A veritable sensation was caused by the frescoes discovered on the walls of the Church of the Intercession in Pskov, which was almost completely buried in 1701 in the course of fortification work. Dating to the mid-fourteenth century, they revealed another vivid chapter in the history of Russian fresco painting. The department also has in its possession fragments of a twelfth-century ornamental painting from Kiev, a set of frescoes from the Church "on the Stream" in Smolensk excavated in 1962–63 (late twelfth and early thirteenth centuries), and a number of others.

The comparatively modest collection of Russian icon painting (about 1,000 pieces) boasts a number of excellent thirteenth- to eighteenth-century icons among which those included in the present book are especially interesting: St. Nicholas (thirteenth century) and Sts. Theodore Stratelates and Theodore the Recruit (fifteenth century), both of the Novgorodian school; the Transfiguration (sixteenth century) of the Tver school; the "northern-style" icons which often carry inscriptions, dates and the names of the artist and donor concerned, such as the icon of St. John the Theologian in Silence by Nektary Kuliuksin (1679).

The collection of Old Russian applied art contains rare specimens of fifteenth-century needlework; gold and silver items with chased and engraved ornamentation, precious stones and enamel; household articles executed with great artistry (caskets, portable lanterns, tin and copper utensils, printed calicos, etc.). Other items likely to attract the visitor's attention include dippers reminiscent of a waterfowl, and *bratinas*—drinking vessels that were usually passed round the table. Vessels of this kind were in use in Russia alone. Especially interesting are the items produced by seventeenth-century craftsmen from Solvychegodsk: various silver and copper bowls, goblets, bottles, and other wares almost entirely covered with vivid ornamentation in the painted enamel technique. This is a uniquely Russian handicraft; there are no analogues in any other country.

Recent years have seen a significant increase in the number of manuscripts and incunabula in the department's collection. Outstanding among these are a fifteenth-century illuminated lectionary, a 1672 manuscript *Title-book* and a number of books produced by the first Russian printer Ivan Fiodorov.

The richest and most representative part of the collection reflects the evolution of Russian culture in the eighteenth and nineteenth centuries: in addition to painting, sculpture, and drawing, the various fields of applied art are also amply illustrated—pottery, metalware, textiles, furniture, and engraved gems.

The collection of paintings—about 3,000—is noteworthy for the singular selective principle on which it is based. It includes portraits of statesmen, scientists, writers, military leaders, and artists: works which have great historical and cultural significance and "everyday" portraits of ordinary Russian people from all walks of life. Large-size battle paintings reflect the Russian people's heroic past. Numerous landscapes and a series of canvases depicting palace interiors are interesting not only as works of art but also as documents bearing on the culture of their time. Among the painters represented are such outstanding masters as Ivan Nikitin, Ivan Argunov, Vladimir Borovikovsky, Karl Briullov, Alexei Venetsianov, Vasily Tropinin, Nikolai Gay, and other talented though lesser known Russian artists.

The section of graphic works numbers about 8,000 drawings and watercolours; among the artists represented are Sylvester Shchedrin, Fiodor Alexeyev, Andrei Martynov, Karl Beggrov, Alexander Orlovsky, Orest Kiprensky, and Sokrat Vorobyov. Of inestimable historic value is a unique gallery of portraits depicting many of those who took part in the Decembrist uprising of 1825 and views of their places of imprisonment and exile in Siberia, including drawings and watercolours by the Decembrists themselves—Nikolai Bestuzhev, Alexander Muravyov, Nikolai Repin, and others. There are also a number of drawings and drafts by major Russian architects—Vasily Bazhenov, Ivan Starov, Nikolai Lvov—and by foreign masters who worked in Russia for many years—Giacomo Quarenghi, Charles Cameron, Antonio Rinaldi, and others.

The collection of prints—engravings and lithographs of the eighteenth to the early twentieth century—is one of the largest in the country and so comprehensive as to allow the viewer to trace the evolution of engraving in Russia over a period exceeding two centuries. The nucleus consists of a collection of prints which since the eighteenth century have been housed in the Hermitage's Print Room. Significantly augmented in Soviet times, the collection of Russian graphics now numbers

35,000 sheets. There are, moreover, about 40,000 prints depicting the military uniforms of the countries of the world, Russia included. A separate group of prints consists of views of St. Petersburg and Moscow—prints executed from drawings by Mikhail Makhayev, Andrei Ukhtomsky, and Stepan Galaktionov, which depict views of suburban palaces at Peterhof, Pavlovsk, and Tsarskoye Selo, and coloured prints by Ivan Chesky, Gabriel and Mathias Lori, and Karl Briullov.

The collection of sculpture, though not very large in size, boasts pieces by such well-known Russian masters as Fiodor Shubin, Mikhail Kozlovsky, Boris Orlovsky, and Fiodor Tolstoi. Special mention must be made of an assortment of works dating to the early eighteenth century which ushered in a new phase in the development of Russian sculpture: two busts by Carlo Bartolomeo Rastrelli (of Peter the Great and Alexander Menshikov), and a large group of low reliefs in bronze and chased copper.

The collection of Russian applied art in the Hermitage ranks among the best in the country. There are over 11,000 items in the porcelain section alone—wares produced at the former Imperial (now the Lomonosov) Porcelain Factory (among them pieces created by Dmitry Vinogradov, the father of Russian porcelain) and at the private factories of Gardner, Popov, Miklashevsky, and Safonov. The Hermitage is famous for its extensive collection of large decorative vases with reproductions of well-known paintings, various items of tableware, and porcelain figurines.

The collection of Russian artistic glass (over 3,000 pieces) consists of items produced by the Izmailovo and Jamburg factories in the late seventeenth and early eighteenth centuries, the St. Petersburg Glass Works which was founded in the 1730s and whose output enjoyed a world reputation, and, finally, of singularly-shaped articles put out by various small glass foundries (belonging, for example, to the Maltsev and Bakhmetyev families). Special mention must be made of coloured glass which first appeared in the mid-eighteenth century after the great Russian scientist Lomonosov invented a new method of colouring the vitreous mass. Coloured-glass articles, which were very popular in the second quarter of the nineteenth century, never fail to impress by their beauty, their refined forms, the richness of their colours, and the elegance of their gold and silver decor.

The department's collection boasts an excellent assortment of gold and silver objects dating from the late seventeenth to the early twentieth century. The silver-ware is so diverse in origin (coming from factories in St. Petersburg, Moscow, Vologda, Tobolsk, Yaroslavl, and other cities) that one can easily follow the changes that occurred in the decor and the processing of the metal in the course of more than two centuries. In addition to household articles, there is a large variety of presentation goblets, dippers, and plates, often with ornate inscriptions in Old Russian honouring this or that historic event. Many of the articles carry the signatures of recognized masters, Russians as well as foreigners, who worked in Russia for many years: Piotr Semionov, Nikolai Don, Illarion Artemyev, Ivan Liebmann, Just Lund, Vasily Sorokin, Zakhary Deichmann, and many others. Another interesting group is nielloed silver by craftsmen from Moscow, Veliky Ustiug, and Tobolsk. The articles on display are good examples of the uniquely Russian technique of processing the surface of the object.

The Russian Baroque in decorative art is beautifully represented by the monumental silver sarcophagus of Alexander Nevsky, an outstanding statesman and military leader of Old Russia. It was made at the St. Petersburg Mint in 1747–52 from metal mined in the Altai region (90 *poods* or 1,440 kilograms of silver went into its making). The huge sarcophagus, the large three-tiered pyramid, the two pedestals adorned with trophies, and the two candelabra are lavishly decorated with chased and engraved scenes, ornamental patterns, and inscriptions; the pyramid is crowned with a chased depiction of Alexander Nevsky himself and his monogram.

The jeweller's art of the second half of the nineteenth and the early twentieth century is represented by the works of whole families of well-known masters, such as Sazikov, Ovchinnikov, Grachov, and Semionov, as well as by the creations of Fabergé, a jeweller's firm of world renown. Characteristic of this period are refined forms and decor, a subtle feel for the material, a predilection for ornamental minerals, especially the famous semiprecious stones from the Urals and Siberia, and the use of coloured enamels.

The pride of the Hermitage is a collection of works by the renowned craftsmen of Tula: the richest in the world, it numbers 300 items out of the 500 currently known (the rest are housed in various Soviet and European museums). Especially valuable are the signed works of Rodion Leontyev, Yevtei Guryanov, and Andrian Sukhanov. The Tula craftsmen produced a decorative effect in their wares by combining silver polished to a mirror sheen or the burnished surface of steel with gilt bronze. Most often, however, they covered their articles with hundreds of cut steel "heads", faceted like diamonds and then polished to create an impression of sparkling gems. The caskets and the samovar reproduced here are excellent examples of Tula craftsmanship.

In the non-precious metal collection of bronze, steel, iron, and cast-iron articles it is the illuminants that deserve special mention: chandeliers, candelabra, candlesticks, and brackets in which bronze often went together with crystal tear-drop pendants.

The collection of coloured stones is justly considered the best in the Soviet Union: the Hermitage is often referred to as a treasure-house of Russian minerals. A significant part of the collection consists of items employing lapis-lazuli with its subtle shades of blue; monochromatic or "patterned" jasper, marble, agate, and porphyry; cherry-pink, black-veined *orlets* stone, and many others. The decorative vases, floor lamps, table-tops, bowls, and obelisks were made at the lapidary works of Peterhof (near St. Petersburg), Kolyvan (in the Altai region) and Ekaterinburg (in the Urals). Objects produced by the major carvers of their day Stepan Morin, Firs and Gavrila Nalimov, Vasily and Yakov Kokovkin, Nikolai and Filipp Strizhov won many awards at various world fairs. The works of these masters stand out for the nobleness of their forms and the subtle elegance of their finish.

The malachite group of the collection is very rich in quantity and quality alike. Malachite is an intricately patterned green stone which came into fashion in the 1830s and '40s, with the discovery of large deposits of the mineral in the Urals. In making malachite articles, huge vases included, the craftsmen usually employed the Russian mosaics technique. Little thin laminae were selected for matching design and colour and affixed to a specially prepared base. The beauty of the resulting pattern depended on the taste and talent of the master. Very often these items were embellished with gilt bronze. One of the reception halls of the Winter Palace has just such a finish—the Malachite Hall where the malachite of the columns, pilasters, and capitals blends harmoniously with the gilding of the ceilings, doors, and architectural details, with the crimson upholstery of the furniture, and with the curtains.

The collection of folk crafts was formed and grew to its present size mainly in the last twenty years. Today it contains textiles, embroidery, pottery, items of wood and bone, and other samples of the traditional handicrafts.

The centuries-old art of Kholmogory bone-carvers is represented in the collection by some of their rarest specimens. These works are truly to be admired for the intricacy and precision of their openwork carving and the expressiveness of the relief scenes or portrait likenesses.

There are over 12,000 items in the department's collection of Russian furniture from the late seventeenth to the early twentieth century, which makes it one of the most extensive in the Soviet Union. Housed in the Hermitage are suites done from drawings by the famous architects Charles Cameron, Giacomo Quarenghi, Carlo Rossi, Vasily Stasov, Luigi Rusca, as well as pieces produced by the well-known St. Petersburg cabinet-makers Christian Meier, the Gambses, Andrei Tur, Nikolai Starchikov, Vasily Bobkov, and others. In addition to palace and manor furniture there are samples of furniture used by the merchant class and some very rare specimens dating to the seventeenth and eighteenth centuries.

All these collections are being constantly studied and popularized. Over the years members of the Hermitage staff have prepared and published numerous catalogues and several illustrated volumes devoted to Russian furniture, tapestries, porcelain, silver, art objects in steel by Tula craftsmen, etc.

The Hermitage keeps the best works of Russian art on permanent display. The materials of the exhibition are so arranged as to clearly and convincingly reflect the interconnection between the various cultural phenomena and the achievements of the Russian people in the fields of fine arts, architecture, literature, education, science, and technology.

Many works of Russian art have been shown in France, Japan, Finland, the USA, the Federal Republic of Germany, and other countries.

Galina Komelova

215. Icon: *St. Theodore Stratelates and St. Theodore the Recruit*

Novgorod. 15th century
Tempera on wood. 535 × 38 cm
Received in 1957 through the Hermitage Purchasing Commission. Inv. No.
ЭРИ-246

Clear silhouettes of slightly elongated figures with comparatively small heads which are set off against the golden background and exquisite colouristic combination of brown, red, golden, and green shades reflect the features characteristic of the Novgorod icon painting of the fifteenth century.

216, 217. Icon: *The Virgin*

Moscow. Late 15th—early 16th century
Tempera on wood. 106 × 89 cm
Received before 1941 from the State Museum Reserve. Inv. No. ЭРИ-55

The special features of this icon from the Deesis are its monumental and solemn quality, the poetic elegance and gentleness typical for portraying the Virgin in ancient Russian art, the generalized treatment of the figure, and the harmony of colours based on rhythmical interchanges of golden and green, and red and blue colours.

15

215

217

NEKTARY KULIUKSIN

218. Icon: *St. John the Theologian in Silence*

Workshop of the Kirillo-Beloziersk Monastery. 1679
Tempera on wood. 109 × 85 cm
An inscription on the reverse says that the icon was painted by Nektary
Kuliuksin, a monk of St. Cyril's Monastery, for the Trinity Church in the
year 188 (?) on December 10.
Received in 1960 (found in the Trinity Church of the Nenoksa village,
Arkhangelsk Region, by the Hermitage expedition). Inv. No. ЭРИ-475

St. John the Theologian is touching his lips with one hand (sign of the vow
of silence), his other hand on the open Gospels; behind him is an angel with
an eight-pointed halo (sign of God's wisdom).

218

219. Icon: *St. Nicholas with Scenes from His Life*

Moscow. Early 16th century
Tempera on wood. 61.5 × 48.5 cm
Received in 1952 through the Hermitage Purchasing Commission. Inv. No.
ЭРИ-84

The veneration of St. Nicholas as the patron saint of Russia was widespread in Old Russian painting. The composition of this icon is typical for icons of this kind—in the centre is the figure of St. Nicholas, surrounding it are fourteen border scenes.

221

NIKOLAI ARGUNOV. 1771–after 1829

221. Portrait of Praskovia Kovaliova-Zhemchugova. *Ca.* 1797

Oil on canvas. 71.5 × 58 cm
Received in 1941 from the Museum of Ethnography of the Peoples of the USSR, Leningrad. Inv. No. ЭРЖ-1885

Nikolai Argunov, son of a well-known Russian portrait painter Ivan Argunov (1768–1803), was a serf of Count Sheremetev.
Praskovia Kovaliova was a daughter of a serf blacksmith. Possessing a rare acting talent, she was a leading singer of the opera house made of serfs belonging to the Counts Sheremetev. Her scenic name was Zhemchugova. In 1801 she became the wife of Count Nikolai Sheremetev.

LOUIS CARAVACQUE (?). 1684–1754

220. Portrait of Natalia Petrovna

Oil on canvas. 115 × 82.5 cm
Received in 1946 through the Hermitage Purchasing Commission. Inv. No. ЭРЖ-1859

Louis Caravacque, a well-known French portraitist and decorator, worked in St. Petersburg from 1716 to the end of his life.
Natalia Petrovna (1718–1725) was the daughter of Peter the Great; after 1721, the tsesarevna.

BENJAMIN PATERSSEN.
1750–1815

222. Sadovaya Street near St. Nicholas' Cathedral in St. Petersburg

Oil on canvas. 68 × 86 cm
Signed bottom right: *Benj: Paterssen*
Main collection of the Hermitage. Inv. No. ЭРЖ-1906

Born in Sweden, Benjamin Paterssen lived in St. Petersburg for nearly thirty years (from 1787). He executed about a hundred paintings and drawings depicting views of the Russian capital.
Sadovaya Street is one of the main streets of St. Petersburg. To the left of the Catherine Canal is St. Nicholas' Cathedral built by Savva Chevakinsky, a pupil of Bartolomeo Francesco Rastrelli between 1753 and 1762. On the left is the building of the Nikolsky Market.

223

UNKNOWN 18th-CENTURY ARTIST

223. Portrait of Mikhail Lomonosov

Oil on canvas. 87 × 70 cm
Received in 1966 through the Hermitage Purchasing Commission.
Inv. No. ЭРЖ-2646

Mikhail Vasilyevich Lomonosov (1711–1765), a Russian philologist, poet, historian, painter, and scientist, was a man of encyclopaedic interests and abilities. It was on his initiative that Moscow University was founded in 1755.

The portrait by an unknown Russian artist is a replica of the work by the Austrian painter Georg Caspar Prenner who lived in Russia in the mid-eighteenth century.

224

JOHANN-HEINRICH SCHMIDT. 1749–1829

224. Portrait of Alexander Suvorov. 1800

Pastel on parchment. 29.5 × 23.5 cm
Received in 1941 from the Museum of Ethnography of the Peoples of the USSR, Leningrad. Inv. No. ЭРР-3766

Johann-Heinrich Schmidt, a well-known author of pastel portraits, was Court Artist to the Elector of Saxony. He lived in Russia in the 1780s.

The portrait was painted from life in Prague where Suvorov made a short stay on his way back to Russia after the march to Switzerland. It was intended for the Gemäldegalerie in Dresden.

Alexander Vasilyevich Suvorov (1730–1800), a great Russian military leader, had won fame in the Seven Years' War, in the Russo-Turkish wars, and other campaigns which Russia led in the eighteenth century. He defeated the army of the Turkish sultan at Kinburn, Focsani, and at the Rymnik river; he stormed and overpowered the Turkish stronghold of Ismail for which he received the title of count and was given the name of Rymniksky.

In 1799 Suvorov was appointed Commander-in-Chief of the Russian army in North Italy. He defeated Moreau on the Adda, Macdonald at the Trebbia, and Joubert at Novi. His army made a dangerous march over the Alps. For his immense services to the state Suvorov was awarded many orders, given the title of Count Italiysky, and the rank of generalissimo. He wrote a book called *The Knack to Win a Victory*.

UNKNOWN 19th-CENTURY ARTIST

225. Portrait of Anna Filatova. 1840s

Oil on canvas. 89 × 70 cm
Received in 1960 through the Hermitage Purchasing Commission. Inv. No.
ЭРЖ-2514

Anna Filatova, the wife of Piotr Filatov, a Rzhev merchant, is portrayed
in a traditional Russian costume, wearing a *kika* head-dress embroidered
in pearls.

226

PIMEN ORLOV. 1812–1863

226. Portrait of a Lady in a Court-dress

Oil on canvas. 81 × 67 cm

Signed lower left: *П. Орлов* $\frac{18\text{-}35}{16}$

Received in 1941 from the Museum of Ethnography, Leningrad. Inv. No. ЭРЖ-1218

Pimen Orlov, a portrait painter, studied at the Academy of Arts; in 1857 he was elected member of the Academy.

The lady portrayed was a maid-of-honour at the Russian court. She is wearing a dress specially designed for gala court receptions.

YAKOV KAPKOV. 1816–1854

227. Portrait of Alexandra Kutorga

Oil on canvas. 80 × 62 cm
Signed and dated lower right: *Капковъ 1847 годъ*
Received in 1941 from the Museum of Ethnography, Leningrad. Inv. No.
ЭРЖ-2595

Yakov Kapkov was a portraitist and a painter of historical subjects; he studied at the Academy of Arts in the class of Karl Briullov.
Alexandra Kutorga was the wife of M. Kutorga, professor at St. Petersburg University. Her brother, Nikolai Ustrialov, was a well-known Russian historian.

UNKNOWN ARTIST. First half of the 19th century

228. Portrait of Field Marshal Kutuzov. 1812

Watercolour and gouache on ivory. 8 × 6.4 cm (oval)
Presented in 1973 by E. Mollo, a British collector. Inv. No. ЭРР-7766

Mikhail Illarionovich Kutuzov (1745–1813), Russian soldier, distinguished himself in the Turkish war and was appointed in 1805 to the command of the First Army Corps against the French. In 1812 as Field Marshal and Commander-in-Chief he fought Napoleon and won a great victory.

PETER ERNST ROCKSTUHL. 1764–1824

229. Portrait of Alexander Ostermann-Tolstoi. Early 1800s

Gouache and grisaille on cardboard. 13 × 10.8 cm (oval)
Main collection of the Hermitage. Inv. No. ЭРР-7750

Rockstuhl worked in Wilno and later, from the 1790s, in St. Petersburg. He painted a great number of profile portraits imitating antique cameos. In the 1810s he executed a whole series of monochromatic portraits on crystal glass ware produced at the St. Petersburg Glass Works.
Alexander Ivanovich Ostermann-Tolstoi (1770–1857), Russian general, distinguished himself in the war of 1812–14.

PIOTR SOKOLOV. 1791–1848

230. Portrait of Alexandra Muravyova. 1825–26

Watercolours on paper. 14.6 × 11.2 cm (oval)
Inscribed on the reverse of the passe-partout: *Pour mon cher Nikita*
Received in 1954 from the Museum of the October Revolution, Leningrad.
Inv. No. ЭРР-5271

Alexandra Muravyova (1804–1832) was the wife of the Decembrist Nikita Muravyov, a distinguished member of the North Society. Her portrait was smuggled to him in the Peter and Paul Fortress on January 5, 1826, where he was imprisoned after the abortive Decembrist insurrection. Later, during Muravyov's exile in Siberia, the portrait was kept with his family.

227

232

PAVEL IVANOV. 1776–1813

231. Portrait of Mikhail Speransky. 1806

Watercolour and gouache on ivory. 7.5 × 6.3 cm (oval)
Main collection of the Hermitage. Inv. No. ЭРР-7753

Pavel Ivanov, a miniaturist, was a pupil of Piotr Zharkov in his class of enamel painting at the Academy of Arts; in 1802 he was elected member of the Academy. Ivanov painted mainly portraits and biblical subjects.
Mikhail Speransky (1772–1839) was an eminent statesman and a jurist. The information concerning the attribution and dating of the portrait was supplied by the historian Mikhail Korf, Speransky's secretary and personal friend.

GRIGORY MUSIKIYSKY. 1670/71–after 1739

232. Portrait of Peter the Great with Trinity Square and Peter and Paul Fortress in the Background. 1723

Gold and enamel. 6.5 × 8.8 cm (oval)
Inscribed left, on the gun barrel, *ГМ* (the artist's monogram), and *Санкт Питербурхъ* (St. Petersburg)
Received in 1941 from the Museum of Ethnography, Leningrad (formerly in the collection of Catherine II in the Winter Palace, later in the Gallery of Peter the Great in the Hermitage). Inv. No. ЭРР-3823

Grigory Musikiysky is one of the first Russian miniature painters to utilize the enamel technique. Seventeen signed miniatures of this master are known at present, six of which are in the Hermitage collection.

233

BARTOLOMEO CARLO RASTRELLI.
1675–1744

233. Bust of Peter the Great. 1723–30

Cast in bronze and chased. 102 × 90 × 40 cm
Received in 1848 from the Academy of Arts, St. Petersburg.
Inv. No. ЭРСк-162

Bartolomeo Carlo Rastrelli was an Italian sculptor who lived and worked in St. Petersburg from 1716 to the end of his life. He is the author of the famous equestrian statue of Peter the Great in Leningrad, the sculptural group representing the Empress Anna Ioannovna with a Negro boy, as well as many portraits and reliefs depicting episodes from Russo-Swedish campaigns.

Peter the Great (1672–1725), the son of Tsar Alexei Mikhailovich, was in 1682–89 a joint-ruler of Russia along with his step-brother Ivan. He was proclaimed Tsar in 1689, and Emperor in 1721.

The bust by Rastrelli is considered to be one of the best portraits of Peter the Great made in his lifetime. The tsar is represented wearing an ermine mantle and armour. On the right breast-plate is depicted an allegorical scene: Peter the Great carving from stone a female figure of Russia.

234

BARTOLOMEO CARLO RASTRELLI. 1675–1744

234. Portrait of Alexander Menshikov. 1716–17

Cast in bronze. 122.5 × 96 × 44 cm
Received in 1977 from the M. Djanchieff collection, Paris. Inv. No. ЭРСк-210

Alexander Menshikov (1673–1729), the closest collaborator of Peter the
Great, was an outstanding politician and had the rank of generalissimo. He
was the first governor-general of St. Petersburg and the President of the
War Department.

236

235. Goblet shaped as ship. *Ca.* 1706

Cast in silver, forged, chased, carved, gilt, and painted. 30.5 × 12 × 37 cm
Engraved on the stern: *1706 повелением великаго императора росíйскаго Петра Алексíевича сыскана серебряная метал всибири вдаурскоí провинцыí спервой перуфикацíи серебра зделан сеи корабль* (In 1706 by the order of the great Emperor of Russia Peter Alexeyevich was found this silver in Siberia, Dauria Province, from the first standard of which silver this ship is made). Inscribed below: *Der Suedn Baum*
Received in 1941 from the Museum of Ethnography, Leningrad. Inv. No. ЭРО-6828

The cup, shaped as a single-masted naval ship, was made of the first standard silver extracted in the Nerchinsk region. It was presented to Peter the Great in 1706.

236. Presentation dipper

Moscow. 1744
Silver, cast, chased, engraved, and gilt. Length 26.2 cm
Hallmark on the handle: $\frac{IA}{B}$ and a 25-copeck coin of 1743 with a portrait of Elizabeth Petrovna
Inscribed along the rim, in two large and six small scrolls: *Бжиею млстию мы елисавет первая императърица и самодержица всероссийская и прочая и прочая и прочая пожаловали симъ ковшемъ воиска донского старшину михаила аркошерина за его верь ныя службы 1744 го июля 28 дня* (By the mercy of God, we, Elizabeth the First, Empress and Autocrat of All Russias etc., presented this dipper to Mikhail Arkosherin, a sergeant of the Don Cossack Army, for his faithful service on July 28, 1744).
Received in 1941 from the Museum of Ethnography, Leningrad. Inv. No. ЭРО-4608

Eighteenth-century presentation dippers differ from earlier ones in that they are more richly ornamented.

CARL LUDWIG

237. Senate (Petrovskaya) Square with the Equestrian Statue of Peter the Great ("The Bronze Horseman"). 1799

Outline engraving and watercolour. 49 × 63 cm (plate, print border not distinct)
Main collection of the Hermitage. Inv. No. ЭРГ-17333

In the centre is the equestrian statue of Peter the Great created by the well-known French sculptor Etienne-Maurice Falconet in 1768–78 (the head of Peter was sculptured by Marie Anne Collot). The pedestal was made of a huge granite rock and the railings around the monument were built to the design of the architect Yuri Velten. On the left is the old building of the Senate. On the right, across the Neva, is the Academy of Fine Arts.

La Statue équestre de

Dedié à SA MAJESTÉ L'EMPEREUR

gravé par C. A. Ludwig 1799

PIERRE I, avec les environs

ET AUTOCRATEUR de toutes les Russies.

239

239. Round dish

Village of Gorbunovo, Moscow Province. Mid-19th century.
The Popov Factory
Porcelain, painted in colours. Diameter 44 cm
Mark in underglaze blue: *ЕП*
Received in 1956 through the Hermitage Purchasing Commission.
Inv. No. ЭРФ-6949

In the nineteenth century, privately-owned factories held a leading position in the production of porcelain. The Popov Factory put out a great variety of household and decorative table-ware distinguished by elegant modelling, bright colours, and profuse ornamentation.

238. Vase with lid

St. Petersburg. Second half of the 18th century.
The Imperial Porcelain Factory
Porcelain, painted in colours. Height 51 cm
Main collection of the Hermitage. Inv. No. ЭРФ-479 а, б

Porcelain articles produced in the second half of the eighteenth century acquired the features of early Russian Classicism. Vases executed during this period are rather modest in size, of widely varying shapes and decor.

240, 241, 242

243

240. Kazan Tartar Woman

St. Petersburg. Second half of the 18th century. The Imperial Porcelain Factory
Porcelain, painted in colours. 22.7 cm
Main collection of the Hermitage. Inv. No. ЭРФ-407

The figurine belongs to the ethnographic series executed in the early 1780s after Johann Georgi's book of engravings entitled *A Description of All the Peoples Inhabiting the Russian State*. The series was executed under the supervision of Jean-Dominique Rachette.

241. Dairywoman

St. Petersburg. Second half of the 18th century. The Imperial Porcelain Factory
Porcelain, painted in colours. Height 19.5 cm
Mark in underglaze blue: $\frac{ЗП}{EII}$
Main collection of the Hermitage. Inv. No. ЭРФ-406

242. Peddler

St. Petersburg. Second half of the 18th century. The Imperial Porcelain Factory
Porcelain, painted in colours. Height 20 cm
Main collection of the Hermitage. Inv. No. ЭРФ-178

This porcelain statuette and the next one belong to the series *Street Vendors and Peddlers of St. Petersburg*, executed in the late 1780s under the supervision of Jean-Dominique Rachette, chief sculptor at the Imperial Porcelain Factory. The figurines present rather idealized images of common people.

243. Casket

Tula. 18th century
Steel, faceted and notched, with applied decorations of gilt bronze.
Height 25 cm
Received in 1972 through the Hermitage Purchasing Commission.
Inv. No. ЭРМ-7771

Tula is the oldest centre of Russian steelwork. The Munition Works established there in 1712 excelled at manufacturing not only arms, but also household articles, such as tables, chairs, caskets, illuminants, etc. Polished steel surface was often inlaid, notched, chased, and gilt. Especially popular was the technique of steel burnishing, resulting in a wide range of shades (from lilac-blue to golden-brown). Very often Tula craftsmen covered their articles with hundreds of cut-steel "heads", faceted like diamonds. Thanks to the combination of exquisite form and original ornamentation with the finest finishing of details, steel objects from Tula have long since won international fame.

244. Tureen with lid. 1799

Silver, gilt and nielloed. Height 30 cm

Hallmarks along the rim: $\frac{1799}{AB}:84°; \frac{AO}{II}$, and emblem of Moscow

Received in 1941 from the Museum of Ethnography, Leningrad. Inv. No. ЭРО-5095

Household silverware of new European types flourished in Russia in the mid-eighteenth century. Tureens like the present one were produced by Moscow, Tobolsk, and Veliky Ustiug silversmiths. Niello technique was often used for embellishing silver articles, the combination of silver, gilding, and niello being extremely impressive.

245. Jug-shaped vase.
First quarter of 19th century

Bronze, patinated and gilt. Height 68.5 cm
Received in 1941 from the Museum of Ethnography, Leningrad. Inv. No. ЭРМ-336

This vase with a handle shaped as a winged woman's figure is supposed to have been executed after a design by Andrei Voronikhin, a famous Russian architect who worked much in the decorative arts. The vase was in all probability made in St. Petersburg. In the first quarter of the nineteenth century the capital of Russia became the main centre of bronzework.

245

247

247. Washing jug with swans

Moscow. 1825. By P. Grigoryev
Silver, embossed and chased. Height 38 cm
Engraved on the bottom: *В Александро-Невскую Лавру от Николая Виктора Дмитрия и Георгия Васильчиковых 1 июня 1878* (To the Alexander Nevsky Monastery from Nikolai, Victor, Dmitry, and Georgy Vasilchkov on June 1, 1878). Hallmarks on the rim: *ПГ,* $\frac{\textit{НД}}{1825}$, *84*, and the emblem of Moscow
Main collection of the Hermitage. Inv. No. ЭРО-4822

This silver jug is a typical specimen of Russian applied art in the period of High Classicism (first quarter of the nineteenth century). The silver articles produced at that time were usually of plain shape; their decor often included ornamental motifs and subject scenes borrowed from the art of Classical Antiquity.

246. Samovar with dolphins

Tula. Late 18th–early 19th century
Steel with applied bronze decorations. Height 87 cm
Main collection of the Hermitage. Inv. No. ЭРМ-2155

A samovar is a typically Russian metal vessel for boiling water. Samovars made in Tula were especially popular all over Russia.

248. Vase. 1840s

Malachite and gilt bronze. Height 68 cm
Received in 1941 from the Museum of Ethnography, Leningrad. Inv. No.
ЭРКМ-326

Malachite, with its rich variety of shades, belongs to the most popular kinds of ornamental stone. Art objects produced by Russian malachite carvers are known the world over.

In the 1830s, when rich deposits of malachite were discovered in the Urals, this semiprecious stone was widely used for making the most diverse articles, from small table ornaments, ink-stands, and clocks to large-size decorative vases, table-tops, and even columns. The technique employed was known as the Russian mosaics: the base of an object, made of some other kind of stone or of metal, was lined with thin (from 3 to 5 mm) laminae of malachite, selected for matching design and colour. It was a common practice to embellish malachite articles with fancy-shaped handles or with sculptured applied decorations of gilt bronze.

248

249. Icon case for the Virgin of Georgia.
Early 19th century

Cloth, embroidered with seed river pearls, silver, gold, and amethysts.
74.5 × 54 cm
Received in 1941 from the Museum of Ethnography, Leningrad. Inv. No.
ЭРТ-9162

Since early times pearl embroidery was used in decorating Russian liturgical vestments, book covers, and icon cases. The intricate vegetal and geometrical motifs often included precious stones, such as amethysts, almandines, or emeralds, whose sparkling colours combined beautifully with the glimmering pearls.

250. Textile fragment

Second half of the 18th century
Silk, embroidered in silver thread. 54 × 74 cm
Main collection of the Hermitage. Inv. No. ЭРТ-18159

The first silk factories in Russia date to the early eighteenth century. By the second half of the same century they were justly famous for the great variety and high quality of fabrics produced. Russian silks of this period are characterized by bright local colours and rich colourful patterns. Gold and silver threads or *chénille* were often woven into the fabric, making the ornamental patterns especially prominent. Silk fabrics were used in making clothes and in decorating palace interiors.

251. "Kolokoltsov" scarf

Serf workshop. First half of the 19th century
Double-woven wool. 225 × 62 cm
Received in 1946. Inv. No. PT-7064

Scarfs and shawls were a fashionable addition to Russian women's costume in the first three decades of the nineteenth century. Especial mastery distinguished the works of serf weavers from the workshops of the landlords Kolokoltsov, Merlina, and Yeliseyeva. Shawls were hand-made of wool of Tibetan goats spinned in threads thinner than a hair and woven in the complex double-sided technique. Unusually bright and festive, these unique specimens of Russian artistic weaving are remarkable for their wealth of floral motifs and the skill of execution.

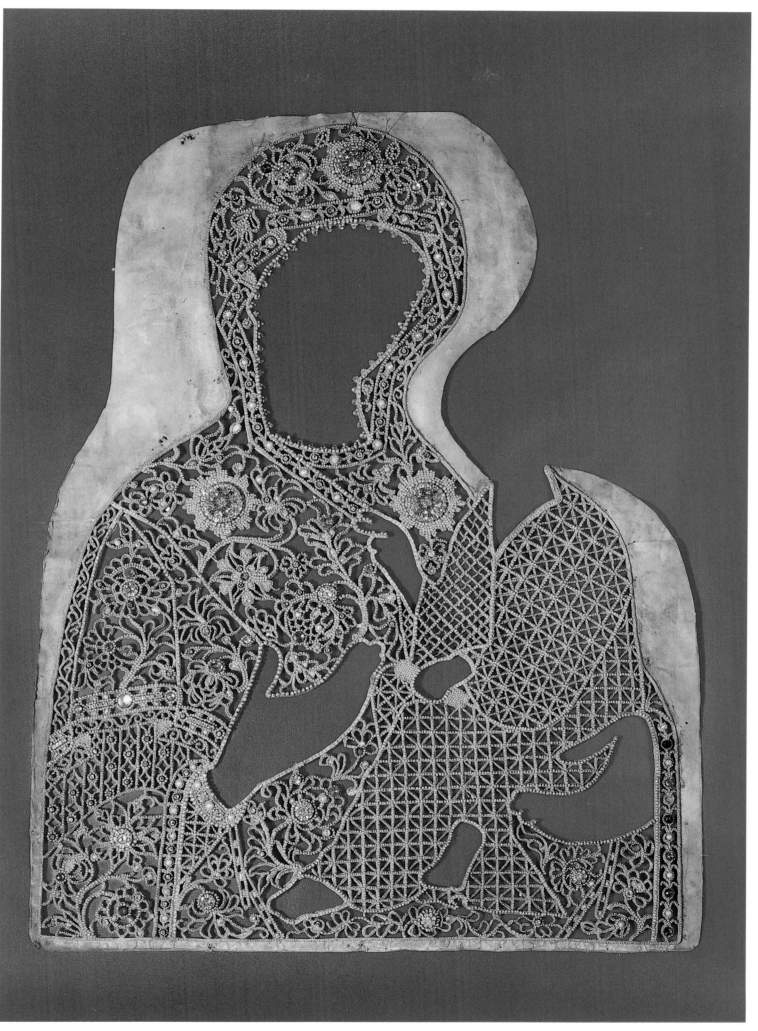

252, 253. Carpet

The St. Petersburg Tapestry Manufactory. 1830s
Hand-woven wool and linen. 265 × 334 cm
Received in 1941 from the Museum of Ethnography, Leningrad. Inv. No.
ЭРТ-12532

The St. Petersburg Tapestry Manufactory was founded in the reign of Peter
the Great, in 1716–17, to make carpets for the decoration of palaces and
mansions in the newly built capital of Russia, as well as for producing
tapestries based on Western European and Russian paintings. The carpets
of the 1830s are characterized by the specific "plafond" design with a
border along the edge and a medallion in the centre, by the wealth of floral
ornamentation, and by bright colour range.

NUMISMATICS

The Numismatics Department of the Hermitage is one of the oldest in the Museum and contains about 1,100,000 pieces. The best examples are on permanent display on the second floor of the Winter Palace.

The collections of the Numismatic Department are well known throughout the Soviet Union and abroad. They include mint cabinets containing classical, Byzantine, Oriental, Western European, and Russian coins; a cabinet for medals and orders; three repositories of which one contains specimens reflecting the 1500-year history of Western European coinage; a collection of numismatic antiquities; and, finally, a library, the best in the country, totalling more than 20,000 volumes on numismatics, sphragistics, heraldry, and genealogy.

The exact date of the foundation of the numismatic collection is unknown, although it is traditionally considered to be 1771, the date of the purchase of the M. Bremsen collection. After this, as documentary evidence shows, further important purchases of numismatic material were made. These acquisitions constituted the so-called *Münzkabinett* (or mint cabinet), which, following the practice customary in the seventeenth and eighteenth centuries, was attached to the library.

In 1864, the Münzkabinett became the Section of Coins and Medals or the Coin Department of the Hermitage. At that time the collection contained approximately 100,000 examples of numismatic art. By 1917 the number of items had increased to more than 250,000. Since the coming of Soviet power, the collection has grown more than fourfold.

From the very first years of the section's existence entire collections and individual rare coins were acquired for it both within the country and abroad. It is enough to mention the J. Reichel collection bought for the Hermitage in St. Petersburg in the mid-nineteenth century; the collection of K. Thieme, acquired in Leipzig in 1906; or the coins obtained from the heirs of the well-known collector Ivan Tolstoi in 1918. The Hermitage was also given great treasures as donations. Another important source in the building up of the Hermitage collection were finds of numismatic material. Many of the ancient coins which came to the Museum with private collections and that of the *Kunstkammer*, or Peter the Great's Cabinet of Curios, derive originally from hoards discovered as early as the late seventeenth and early eighteenth centuries. With the founding of the Imperial Archaeological Commission in 1859, hoards began to enter the Hermitage on a more regular basis. The Museum obtained in this way a number of rare coins, among them the denarius of Florentius I, Count of Holland (1049–61), and the unique dirhem of the Abbasids, minted to commemorate the fiftieth birthday of Subaydah, wife of Haroun al-Raschid.

At present the Numismatics Department consists of the following sections: the Ancient Section, whose collection numbers 130,000 items; the Russian Section, with more than 250,000 coins; the Western European Section, containing over 330,000 coins from both Europe and America; and the Section of Orders, Medals and Badges, with 60,000 various objects in its stocks.

The medals of the Italian Renaissance—the work of Antonio Pisano, Matteo de Pasti, Niccolo Fiorentino, Leone Leoni, and Benvenuto Cellini—are the pride of the Hermitage. There are also about 11,000 items produced by the German medallists Albrecht Dürer, Hans Schwarz, Friedrich Hagenauer, Mattheus Gebel, Hans Reinhart, Valentin Maler, Sebastian Dadler, and others. No less important are other sections. The following figures may give some idea of the richness and variety of the collection of medals: it contains 6,000 French pieces, 1,200 Netherlandish items, and 1,200 medals from England. Of course, Russian medals are most fully represented, with more than 1,200 examples of gold and platinum medals alone.

Soon after its formation, the Numismatics Department of the Hermitage became a centre of scientific research. The staff of the Hermitage combined their activity in the Museum with numismatic work in such scholarly institutions as the Academy of Sciences, the Archaeological Commission, and the University, at the same time maintaining close ties with foreign museums. Quite a number of the department staff are today honorary members of foreign numismatic societies.

Vsevolod Potin

254, 255

256, 257

258, 259

256, 257. Tetradrachm

Athens, Attica. 6th century B.C.
Silver, weight 17.04 g, dia. 24 mm
Provenance unknown. Inv. No. 10183

Obverse: Head of Athena
Reverse: Owl, an attribute of Athena, the goddess of Wisdom and patroness of the city of Athens; olive spray, the symbol of Attica's prosperity
Athens' tetradrachm was one of the most widely circulated coins of antiquity, highly valued for its metal purity and precise weight.

254, 255. Decadrachm

Syracuse, Sicily. 5th century B.C.
Silver, weight 43.95 g, dia. 35 mm
Provenance unknown. Inv. No. 2342

Obverse: Head of Artemis-Arethusa; around, four dolphins
Reverse: Quadriga crowned by Nike, the goddess of Victory; in exergue, a lion
This coin issued to commemorate the Syracusan victory over Athens in the battle at Asinaria is a remarkable specimen of Greek art.

258, 259. Stater

Kyzikos, Mysia. 6th century B.C.
Gold, weight 15.99 g, size 19/16 mm
Provenance unknown. Inv. No. 1197

Obverse: Lion; beneath, tunny fish, the emblem of the city of Kyzikos
Reverse: Quadripartite incuse square

343

260

261, 262

263, 264

265, 266

260—262. Octadrachm

Egypt. Ptolemy II and Arsinoë (285–246 B.C.)
Gold, weight 27.72 g, dia. 26 mm
Provenance unknown. Inv. No. 1400

Obverse: Ptolemy II and Arsinoë
Reserve: Ptolemy I and Berenice I
This piece belongs to the so-called "commemorative" coinage of antiquity remarkable for their high artistic merits.

263, 264. Stater

Olbia. 4th century B.C.
Silver, weight 12.28 g, dia. 24 mm
Received in 1915 from a private collection. Inv. No. 25144

Observe: Head of Demeter
Reverse: Sea-eagle standing on dolphin, the symbol of the city-state of Olbia

Demeter, the goddess of Fertility, symbolizes the prosperity of Olbia, the Graece-Scythian merchant colony on the Northern Black Sea Coast.

265, 266. Stater

Panticapaeum, the Kingdom of Bosporus. 4th century B.C.
Gold, weight 9.06 g, dia. 18 mm
Received in 1925 from the S. Stroganov collection. Inv. No. 630

Observe: Head of satyr
Reverse: Winged, lion-headed griffin holding spear in its mouth; beneath, ear of corn symbolizing prosperity of the Kingdom of Bosporus

267, 268

269, 270

267, 268. Medallion. Five—six aurei

Roman Empire, Numerian (283–284)
Gold, weight 26.97 g, dia. 34 mm
Received in the first half of the 19th century from the S. Stroganov collection. Inv. No. 2090/A-3

Obverse: The emperor, in military raiment, holding the horse by the bridle
Reverse: Carus and Numerian, crowned by winged Victories, contend with the enemy

269, 270. Medallion. Eight solidi

Roman Empire, Constantius II (337–361)
Gold, weight 41.89 g, dia. 49 mm
Received in the late 19th century as part of the Kievo-Pecherskaya Lavra (Monastery) hoard. Inv. No. 2142/A-3

Obverse: The emperor crowned by Victoria
Reverse: Constantius and Constans on triumphal car; beneath, imperial gifts to the army: coffer, sacks with coins, wreaths

271, 272. Medallion. Eight solidi

Roman Empire, Constantine I (306–337)
Gold, weight 43.86 g, dia. 48 mm
Received in 1928 (found during earthworks). Inv. No. 2155/A-3

Obverse: Bust of the emperor
Reverse: Constantine enthroned, surrounded by his sons

271, 272

273, 275, 277
274, 276, 278

273, 274. Denarius

Holland. Florentius I (1049–61)
Silver, weight 0.82 g, dia. 22 mm
Received in 1934 as part of the Vikhmiaz hoard. Inv. No. 3798

Obverse: The ruler holding a banner in his left and an orb in his right hand
Reverse: *BVRCH*, an inscription in the centre of the coin field between the two dotted lines, completing the legend *LETHERIS*. Both inscriptions refer to the place of minting, which was probably Leiden.

275, 276. Denarius

Germany. Hildesheim. Mid-11th century
Silver, weight 1.37 g, dia. 22 mm
Received in 1934 as part of the Vikhmiaz hoard. Inv. No. 7323

Obverse: German Holy Roman Emperor Henry III (1046–56)
Reverse: The church of St. Michael with two tall and two small belfries surmounted by a blessing hand

277, 278. Denarius

Germany. Echternach. Early 11th century
Silver, weight 1.21 g, dia. 21.5 mm
Received in 1934 as part of the Vikhmiaz hoard. Inv. No. 851

Obverse: St. Willibrord, patron-saint of the Echternach abbey
Reverse: *EF-TR-NA-GS*, the name of the place where the coin was struck.

279, 280. Eight ducats. 1528

Germany. Hildesheim
Gold, weight 28.65 g, dia. 47 mm
Received in 1925 from the Stroganov family collection. Inv. No. 1721

Obverse: German Holy Roman Emperor Charles V (1519–56) with the order of the Golden Fleece
Reverse: The oval-shaped arms crowned with a helmet and surmounted by a female figure

279, 280

281, 282

283, 284

281, 282. Ten ducats

Denmark. Christian IV (1588–1648)
Gold, weight 33.54 g, dia. 53 mm
Received in 1925 from the Stroganov family collection. Inv. No. 5848

Obverse: Christian IV, cuirassed, holding a staff
Reverse: Knight on horseback; fourteen oval armorial shields surmounted by a crown; beneath, an elephant

283, 284. Double noble.1496

Denmark
Gold, weight 14.74 g, dia. 39.5 mm
Received before 1917. Inv. No. 5840

Obverse: King enthroned
Reverse: armorial shield surmounted by a crown

285, 286

285, 286. Sovereign

England. Henry VII (1485–1509)
Gold, weight 15.39 g, dia. 39.5 mm
Received in 1858 from the J. Reichel collection. Inv. No. 5678

Obverse: King enthroned
Reverse: The late 15th-century English armorial shield, placed in the centre of a stylized rose

287, 288. Five ducats. 1654

Riga
Gold, weight 17.42 g, dia. 40 mm
Received in 1858 from the J. Reichel collection. Inv. No. 595

Reverse: Panoramic view of the town of Riga surmounted by two lions holding a big coat of arms of the town

287

288

289, 290

291, 292

291, 292. Quadruple testone

France Charles IX (1560–74)
Silver, weight 38.3 g, dia. 32 mm
Received in 1858 from the J. Reichel collection. Inv. No. 150

Obverse: Charles IX, in armour
Reverse: Armorial shield surmounted by a crown
Edge legend, *VERAE RELIGIONIS ASSRTORI* (protector of the true faith), may be referring to the events of the massacre of St. Bartholomew.

289, 290. Four testones

Italy, Savoy. Filiberto, the Duke of Savoy II (1497–1504)
Silver, weight 37.74 g, dia. 45 mm
Received in 1858 from the J. Reichel collection. Inv. No. 24344

Obverse: Filiberto II, the Duke of Savoy
Reverse: Iolanta Lodovica, the first wife of the Duke Filiberto II

354

293, 294

293, 294. Ten ducats.1850

The Great Principality of Lithuania. Stephen Bathory (1516–1586)
Gold, weight 35.67 g, dia. 41 mm
Received in 1899 as part of the Kievo-Pecherskaya Monastery hoard. Inv.
No. 638

Obverse: Stephen Bathory
Reverse: Armorial shield with the Polish and the Lithuanian arms on it surmounted by a crown

295. Half-thaler of Charles I (1516–56)

Silver, weight 14.8 g, dia. 35 mm
Received in 1927 from the reserve of the USSR Academy of Sciences.
Inv. No. 59513

296. Thaler of Philip II (1556–98)

Silver, weight 29.42 g, dia. 41 mm
Received before 1917. Inv. No. 59509

297. Half-thaler of Philip II (1556–98)

Silver, weight 14.55 g, dia. 34 mm
Acquired before 1917. Inv. No. 59510

Neapolitan coins bearing the 1564 countermark of
Sigismund II Augustus, king of Poland (part of his
mother's, the Milanese duchess Bona Sforza, inheri-
tance).

298–300. Ten scudo.1641

Savoy. Karlo Emanuele II (1638–75)
Gold, weight 33.23 g, dia. 44.5 mm
Received in 1925 from the Stroganov family collection. Inv. No. 4668

Obverse: Infant Karlo Emanuele and his mother
Christina
Reverse: Armorial shield surmounted by a crown

298

299, 300

301, 302
303, 304

301. Solidus

Byzantium, Philippicus Bardanes (711–713)
Gold, weight 4.42 g, dia. 20 mm
Received in 1925 from the Stroganov family collection. Inv. No. 3990

302. Semissis

Byzantium, Philippicus Bardanes (711–713)
Gold, weight 2.22 g, dia. 18 mm
Received in 1890 from the Photiades Pasha collection. Inv. No. 3922

303. Tremissis

Byzantium, Philippicus Bardanes (711–713)
Gold, weight 1.42 g, dia. 16 mm
Received in 1890, probably, from the Photiades Pasha collection. Inv. No. 3993

304. Half-tremissis

Byzantium, Philippicus Bardanes (711–713)
Gold, weight 0.73 g, dia. 13 mm
Received in 1931 from the I. Tolstoi collection in the Russian Museum, Leningrad. Inv. No. 4448

The superb workmanship of the engravers is truly remarkable: one cannot but admire the mastery with which they render absolutely identical the representations of the emperor in *loros* and with an orb and a staff in his hands on coins of such different size (ranging in dia. from 20 to 13 mm).

305. Coin

Byzantium. Leontius (695–698)
Silver, weight 0.34 g, dia. 11 mm
Provenance unknown. Inv. No. 3174

The coin was made in the mint of Ravenna.

306, 307. Coin

Byzantium. Justinian II (705–711)
Silver, weight 3.98 g, dia. 20 mm
Received in 1897 from the Prince Lobanov-Rostovsky collection. Inv. No. 3148

Obverse: Emperor Justinian II
Reverse: Christ
This is a "ceremonial" piece reproducing the gold solidus type of the period, with the obverse type showing the emperor holding the regalia in his hands. The representation of Christ on the reverse is the earliest in coinage.

308, 309

310, 311

312

313, 314

315

308, 309. Coin

Cilicia, Rubenids. Leon I (1190–1219)
Gold, weight 6.9 g, dia. 24.5 mm
Provenance unknown. Inv. No. 5154

Obverse: Legend in Armenian
Reverse: Legend in Armenian

310, 311. Dirhem. 810/811

Abbasids
Silver, weight 2.72 g, dia. 24 mm
Received in 1951 as part of the hoard dug out in 1927 near the village of
Shumilovo, Novgorod Region. Inv. No. 9190

Obverse: Legend in Arabic
Reverse: Legend in Arabic
This is a unique commemorative specimen struck on
the occasion of the 50th birthday of Subaydah, wife
of Haroun al-Raschid, and mother of khalif Al-Amin.

312. Fish-shaped coin. 1210

Georgia. Georgi IV Lasha (1213–22)
Copper, weight 18.8 g, length 70 mm
Received before 1917. Inv. No. 14392

The only known Georgian specimen of an odd-shaped
coining.

313, 314. Two dinars

Iran, Sassanids. Hormizd II (302–309)
Gold, weight 14.86 g, dia. 34 mm
Received before 1917 from the I. Bartholomey collection. Inv. No. 191

Obverse: Bust of King Hormizd II
Reverse: Fire altar
This is the only surviving coin of such large denomi-
nation.

315. Dirhem. 642 A.H. (1244/45)

Genghisids. Toragana Khatun 639–644 A.H. (1241–46)
Gandzha
Silver, weight 2.83 g, dia. 21 mm
Received before 1917. Inv. No. 14870

Reverse: Scene of hunting
An anonymous coin struck at a time when the widow
of Ogadai Khan ruled the Golden Horde as regent.

318

319

320, 321

316, 317. Ten dinars (sixty dirhems).
742 A.H. (1341/42)

Hulagu. Abu Sa'id 716–736 A.H. (1316–35)
Tabriz
Silver, 103.65 g, dia. 75 mm
Received before 1917. Inv. No. 28898

Obverse and reverse types
Coins of such a rare denomination were intended as
gifts or rewards.

318. Five krans. 1320 A.H. (1902)

Iran, Kajars. Muzaffar ad-Din, 1314–24 A.H. (1896–1906)
Silver, 23.12 g, dia. 38 mm
Received in 1921 from the Petrograd Mint. Inv. No. 35465

The specimen belongs to a series of Iranian coinage
struck at the Mint of St. Petersburg in the early twentieth century.

319. A die for manual coining. 1279 A.H. (1862/63)

Khahanate of Khiva. Sayyid Mohammed 1272–81 A.H. (1856–65)
Khorezm
Length about 100 mm
The specimen belongs to a unique collection of dies of the Khivan Khaha-
nate brought to St. Petersburg in the late nineteenth century. Inv. No. 85

320, 321. Tanga, the reserve type of which was
struck with the die reproduced on Pl. No. 319

Silver, weight 3.14 g, dia. 20 mm
Received in the early 1900s from the V. Velyaminov-Zernov collection. Inv.
No. 32736

363

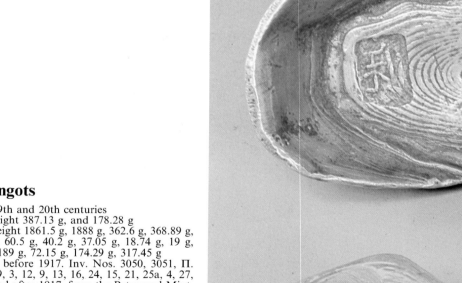

322. Ingots

China, 19th and 20th centuries
Gold, weight 387.13 g, and 178.28 g
Silver, weight 1861.5 g, 1888 g, 362.6 g, 368.89 g,
185.76 g, 60.5 g, 40.2 g, 37.05 g, 18.74 g, 19 g,
356.5 g, 189 g, 72.15 g, 174.29 g, 317.45 g
Received before 1917. Inv. Nos. 3050, 3051, П.
583/196-9, 3, 12, 9, 13, 16, 24, 15, 21, 25a, 4, 27,
54, 28; and after 1917, from the Petrograd Mint,
Inv. No. П. 583/180-5

Traditionally, such ingots were used as raw material by goldsmiths in their work, and in periods of economic instability they served as means of payment.
Silver "sycee" ingots were used in currency circulation, their value depending on weight. i.e. the purity of metal.

御賜
春
老

324

324. Commemorative *p'ai-tzu.* 1785

China. K'ien-lung (1736–96)
Silver,weight 373 g, size 13.8 × 8.5 mm
Received in 1869 from the G. Trub collection. Inv. No. 2391

Obverse: Two dragons in clouds, playing with a blazing pearl. An hieroglyphic inscription in the centre This commemorative piece was handed to one of a thousand venerable old men summoned to an audience in the palace of the Emperor K'ien-lung which was given by him in honour of the elders in the fiftieth year of his rule.

323. Sin-kin oban (new gold oban, which was then a gold coin of the largest size). 1725

Japan
Gold, weight 165.1 g, a rectangle, dimensions 15.5 × 9.5 mm
Received in 1882 as part of a collection of gold and silver coins sent as a gift to the Russian tsar by the government of Japan. Inv. No. 2946

The obverse shows quadrupled national emblem of Japan in the shape of a flower of the Paulownia tree.

325. Zlatnik of the Grand Prince Vladimir Sviatoslavich (*ca.* 980–1015). 988

Kiev
Gold, weight 4.4 g, dia. 23 mm
Received in 1804 as part of the hoard unearthed in the vicinity of the town of Pinsk, Byelorussia.
Inv. No. A3-12

Obverse: The Grand Prince Vladimir Sviatoslavich; over his left shoulder, the princely emblem shaped as trident

326, 327. Srebrenik of Prince Yaroslav the Wise (1019–54). *Ca.* 1015

Novgorod
Silver, weight 3.77 g, dia. 25 mm
Received in 1925 from the S. Stroganov collection, St. Petersburg. Inv. No. 138

Obverse: St. George (patron saint of Prince Yaroslav) with his name inscribed on both sides
Reverse: The princely badge (the arms) of Yaroslav

328, 329. Ducat of Ivan III (1462–1505)

Russia
Gold, weight 3.59 g, dia. 24 mm
Received in 1864 from the town of Riga. Inv. No.A3–19

Observe: St. Vladislav holding a pole-axe and an orb
Reverse: Shield quartered to marshal the arms of Hungary, Matthias Corvinus, and Bohemia

325

326, 327
328, 329

330, 331

332

333

330, 331. Rouble
of Peter the Great (1682–1725). 1704

Russia
Engraver Fiodor Alexeyev
Silver, weight 29.24 g, dia. 44 mm
Received before 1917. Inv. No. 656

Obverse: Peter the Great, in armour
Reverse: Double-headed eagle with each head crowned, holding the sceptre and orb, the whole surmounted by a crown

332. Double chervonets. 1714

Russia, Peter the Great (1682–1725)
Gold, weight 6.95 g, dia. 27 mm
Provenance unknown. Inv. No. Аз–220

Obverse: Peter the Great

333. Pattern imperial (ten roubles) –
Elisabeth d'or. 1755

Russia, tsarina Elizabeth Petrovna (1741–62)
Engraver Benjamin Scott
Gold, weight 16.37 g, dia. 32 mm
Received in the early 1900s from the Belin auctioneers. Inv. No. Аз–451

Obverse: Tsarina Elizabeth Petrovna
The coin is unique as the imperial was not authorized.

334, 335

334, 335. Pattern piatak (five-kopeck piece). 1757

Russia, tsarina Elizabeth Petrovna (1741–62)
Copper, weight 51.05 g, dia. 43 mm
Received in 1917 as part of the I. Tolstoi collection. Inv. No. 7520

Obverse: The arms of St. Petersburg
Reverse: Tsarina's monogram constisting of the mirror images of letters *E*
and *P* surmounted by a crown
The coin was not authorized.

337, 338. Poltina (silver fifty-kopeck piece) struck in platinum. 1826

Russia, Nicholas I (1825–55)
Weight 21.24 g, dia. 28 mm
Provenance unknown. Inv. No. A–пл. 3

Obverse: Double-headed eagle surmounted by the imperial crown
Reverse: Wreath, the imperial crown at top

339. *Sakoma* (Bashkir breast ornament worn by women)

Silver coins, beads of malachite, amethyst, garnet, cornelian and coral
Breadth 35.5 cm
Received in 1949 from the Hermitage Department of the History of Russian Culture. Inv. No. 63749

A total of 612 Russian silver coins were used in producing the ornament. The coins date from the sixteenth to the eighteenth century, the most recent one being the rouble of Peter I struck in 1721.

336. Pattern rouble (the Constantine rouble). 1825

Russia
Engraver Jacob Reichel
Silver, weight 20.63 g, dia. 35.5 mm
Received in 1879 from the archives of the Ministry of Finance along with the dies. Inv. No. 11833

Obverse: Constantine Pavlovich, a younger brother of Tsar Alexander I
The piece is one of the seven coins minted at St. Petersburg Mint when the news of the death of tsar Alexander I (1801–1825) reached the capital. Constantine Pavlovich renounced his rights to the throne in favour of his younger brother Nicholas I.

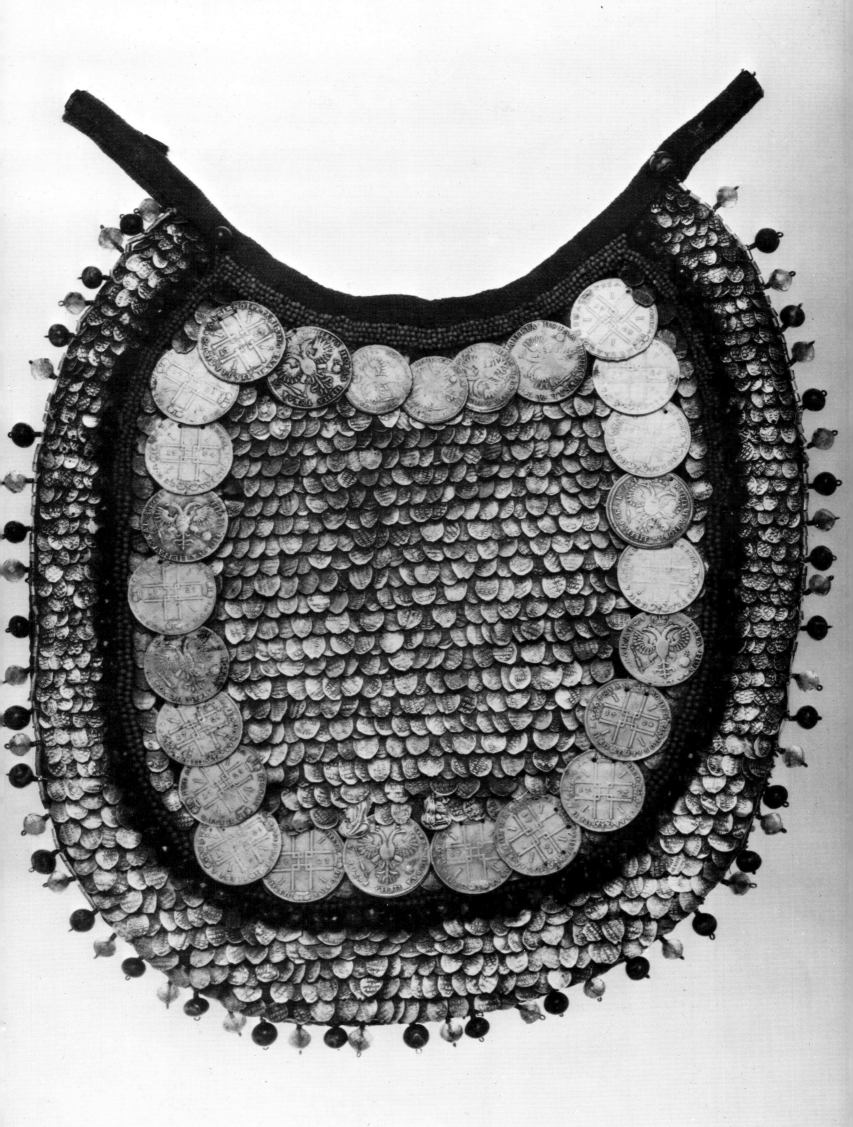

340

PISANELLO (ANTONIO DI PUCCIO PISANO). *Ca.* 1395–1455
Italy

340, 341. Medal: *Lodovico Gonzaga.* 1447–48

Cast in bronze, dia. 101 mm
Received before the mid-19th century. Inv. No. 5169

Reverse: Medallist's signature, *OPVS PISANI PIC-TORIS*
Lodovico Gonzaga (1414–78), second Marquess of Mantua, was Captain General of the Florentines at the time when the medal was cast.

341

343, 344

BENVENUTO CELLINI. 1500–71
Italy

342–344. Medal: *Clement VII.* 1534

Cast in silver, dia. 40 mm
Received before the mid-19th century. Inv. No. 5330

Obverse: Giulio de Medici, pope Clement VII
(1523–34)
Reverse: Moses striking the rock. Inscription, *VT BI-BAT POPVLVS* (May the people be slaked)
The medal was dedicated to the construction of a well
in Orvieto.

MATTEO DE PASTI. Active 1441–68
Italy

345, 346. Medal: *Isotta degli Atti da Rimini.* 1446

Received before the mid-19th century. Inv. No. 5186

Reverse: Above, medallist's signature, *OPVS MAT-HEI DE PASTI*; beneath, the date, *MCCCCXLVI*
Isotta degli Atti da Rimini (died 1474/5) was a mistress
(1446) and later (1456) the third wife of Sigismondo
Pandolpho Malatesta, Lord of Rimini and Fano.

Inscription, *ISOTE ARIMINENSI FORMA ET VIRTVTE ITALIE DECORI* (To Isotta da Rimini, whose looks and virtues are Italy's adornment). The Malatesta elephant on the reverse is the emblem of the house of Rimini, symbolizing force and virtue.

THE MANNER OF NICCOLO FIORENTINO. 1430–1514
Italy

347, 348. Medal: *Girolamo Savonarola. Ca.* 1497

Cast in copper, dia. 62 mm
Received before the mid-19th century. Inv. No. 5266

Obverse: Girolama Savonarola (1452–98), Dominican
preacher, religious and political reformer in late fif-teenth-century Florence
Reverse: Legend, the text from Savonarola's sermon,
GLADIVS. DOMINI. SVP. TERAM. CITO. ET VE-LOCITER. (Sword of the Lord is overhead, soon and
speedy)

345,

348

349, 350

UNIDENTIFIED MEDALLIST

France

349, 350. Medal: *Charles VII.* 1455

Cast in silver and gilt, dia. 51 mm
Received in 1858 from the J. Reichel collection. Inv. No. 30853

Charles VII, the King of France (1422–61).
The medal was dedicated to the expulsion of the English from France. With the king's name and his title given in full, the both sides of the medal are close in their design and legend to those of armorial seals.

UNIDENTIFIED MEDALLIST

France

351, 352. Medal: *Antoine, the Duke of Lorraine, and Renée de Bourbon.* 1520–30

Cast in silver, dia. 41 mm
Received in 1858 from the J. Reichel collection. Inv. No. 17731

353

354

GERMAIN PILLON. *Ca.* 1535–90

France

353. Medal: *Henry III.* 1575

Cast in bronze and silver-plated, dia. 160 mm
Received in 1918 from the Winter Palace collection. Inv. No. 100

Henry III Valois (1551–89), was elected to the crown of Poland in 1573, and in 1575 succeded his brother, Charles IX, on the French throne.
The medallion belongs to the *Les Valois* series created by Pillon in 1573–77.

ALBRECHT DÜRER. 1471–1528

Germany

354. A single-faced medal with a female head (the so-called "Lucretia") on the obverse

16th-century lead casting made from a wax model, dia. 54 mm
To the left and right of the representation, the artist's monogram and the date: *1508*
Acquired in 1858 from a Genevan antique dealer Soret. Inv. No. 17696

The terse artistic manner and the pithiness of the barely outlined relief call to mind the best graphic works of the master from his mature period.

357, 358

FRIEDRICH HAGENAUER. Active 1525–43

Germany

355, 356. Medal: *Johann von Theven.* 1544

Cast in lead, dia. 58 mm
Received in 1925 from the S.G. Stroganov collection. Inv. No. 17744

Obverse: Medallist's monogram *FH* to the right of the portrait
Johann von Theven (1506–77) was the chief Treasurer of the municipality of Cologne
Reverse: *SALVS POPVLI SVPREMA LEX EST* (People's Welfare is the Supreme Law)
The medal is unique.

VALENTIN MALER. Active 1563–95

Germany

357, 358. Medal commemorating the flood of 1595

Cast in silver and gilt, dia. 36 mm
Received before the mid-19th century. Inv. No. 17915

Reverse: in exergue, medallist's monogram *V.M.*
The event commemorated by the medal is rendered here through the mythological personae: that of Fortune, goddess of destiny, and a river deity supporting a ship.

359

UNIDENTIFIED ARTIST.
Late 16th – early 17th centuries

The Ukraine

359. Medal: *Konstantin Ostrozhsky*

Cast in gold, dia. 48 mm
Received in 1889 as part of the Kievo-Pecherskaya
Monastery hoard. Inv. No. A-3 1524

Konstantin Ostrozhsky (1526–1608), a Ukrainian
magnate, was a prominent figure in the Ukrainian
Enlightenment. It was through his financial aid that
the first Russian printer Ivan Fiodorov established the
printing press at the town of Ostrog.

JACOB JONGHELINCK. 1530–1606

The Netherlands

360, 361. Medal: *Charles Philip de Croy.* 1601

Cast in silver, dia. 44 mm
Received before the mid-19th century. Inv. No. 26652

Charles Philip de Croy, marquess de Havre (1549–
1613), was a stadholder of the Spanish Netherlands
Reverse: The shield, within a collar of the Order of the
Golden Fleece and surmounted by a crown; the Mot-
to, *SANS FIN CROY* (Infinitely Loyal), and date,
1601

360, 361

THOMAS SIMON (?).
1618–1665
England

362. Medal issued for participants of a naval engagement of July 31, 1650

Struck in silver, oval, 34 × 47 mm
Received in the mid-19th century as part of the *Kunstkammer* collection. Provenance: the private collection of Peter the Great. Inv. No. 7382

Obverse: An anchor from the beams of which are suspended the shields of England and Ireland. Above, *MERUISTI* (Thou hast merited)
A rare specimen of the early campaign medals. The medal was instituted by order of the British Parliament as a reward for the crewmen of the British ship who under Captain Wyard beat off six Irish frigates on the night of July 31, 1650.

JEAN DU VIVIER. 1687–1761
MARTIN ROEG. 1685–1736
France

363, 364. Medal: *Peter the Great Visiting the Paris Mint in 1717*

Cast in silver, dia. 60 mm
Received in the mid-19th century as part of the *Kunstkammer* collection. Inv. No. 662

Obverse: signature, *DU VIVIER*, on the truncation of arm
Reverse: Glory sounding the trumpet. Legend, *VIRES ACQUIRIT EUNDO* (Striding forth he augments his power)
During Peter the Great's visit to the Paris Mint in May 1717, a few medals were struck for the occasion. The gold specimen, struck in his presence, was handed to the tsar; the silver ones were presented to persons of the tsar's entourage.

363, 364

365, 366

GOTTFRIED HAUPT. Active 1706–14

Russia

**365, 366. Campaign medal for colonels.
Battle of Kalicz, October 18, 1706**

Struck in gold
The oval gold medal measuring 39 × 43 mm is contained in a gold frame surmounted by a crown, decorated with enamel and studded on the obverse with diamonds and aquamarines. Size (with mount) 94 × 55 mm
Acquisition date unknown. Inv. No.B-з 332

Obverse: On the truncation of arm, medallist's monogram *H*
Reverse: Peter I, on a rearing horse, commanding the battle
The victory at Kalicz was the first occasion in the Russian history in honour of which officers were awarded gold medals on a mass scale, the size and weight of the medal depending strictly on rank.

JOHANN BALTHASAR GASS. 1730–1813

Russia

367, 368. Medal: *Alexei Orlov.* 1770

Struck in gold, dia. 91 mm
Acquired by the library of the Winter Palace in 1771. Inv. No. A-з 1009

Obverse: in exergue, medallist's signature, *I. B. GASS*
Reverse: The view of the two fleets in action
The medal is dedicated to the victory of the Russian fleet over the Turks in the naval engagement at Chesme Bay on 24 to 26 June 1770
Alexei Grigoryevich Orlov (1737–1808) was the Commander-in-Chief of the Russian army during the Russo-Turkish War of 1768–70 on land and at sea.
Besides Alexei Orlov, the gold medal bearing his portrait was handed to Admiral Grigory Spiridov, the genuine victor of the Chesme Battle.